Information Systems

Achieving Success by Avoiding Failure

Information Systems

Achieving Success by Avoiding Failure

by

JOYCE FORTUNE

GEOFF PETERS

John Wiley & Sons, Ltd

Other Wiley Editorial Offices

John Wiley & Sons Inc., 111 River Street, Hoboken, NJ 07030, USA

Jossey-Bass, 989 Market Street, San Francisco, CA 94103-1741, USA

Wiley-VCH Verlag GmbH, Boschstr. 12, D-69469 Weinheim, Germany

John Wiley & Sons Australia Ltd, 33 Park Road, Milton, Queensland 4064, Australia

John Wiley & Sons (Asia) Pte Ltd, 2 Clementi Loop #02-01, Jin Xing Distripark, Singapore 129809

John Wiley & Sons Canada Ltd, 22 Worcester Road, Etobicoke, Ontario, Canada M9W 1L1

Wiley also publishes its books in a variety of electronic formats. Some content that appears
in print may not be available in electronic books.

Library of Congress Cataloging-in-Publication Data

Fortune, Joyce.
    Information systems : achieving success by avoiding failure / by Joyce
Fortune, Geoff Peters.
        p. cm.
    Includes bibliographical references and index.
    ISBN 0-470-86255-6 (pbk.)
    1. System failures (Engineering) 2. System safety. 3.
Accidents – Prevention.   I. Peters, Geoff. II. Title.
    TA169.5.F65 2005
    658.4'032 – dc22

                                            2004020583

British Library Cataloguing in Publication Data

A catalogue record for this book is available from the British Library

ISBN 0-470-86255-6

Typeset in 10pt/15pt Sabon by Laserwords Private Limited, Chennai, India
Printed and bound in Great Britain by TJ International, Padstow, Cornwall
This book is printed on acid-free paper responsibly manufactured from sustainable forestry
in which at least two trees are planted for each one used for paper production.

Dedication

To Benedict and Lucy
and Gemma, Alexis and Anna

CONTENTS

ABOUT THE AUTHORS

Dr Joyce Fortune

Joyce Fortune is a Senior Lecturer and Head of the Department of Technology Management at the Open University. Her teaching and research interests include systems failures, quality management and technology strategy. Her most recent papers have covered a wide range of topics including risk in project management, human rights and ethical policing, emergence and systems approaches to failure. This is her third book on systems failures.

Professor Geoff Peters

Geoff Peters is Professor of Systems Strategy at the Open University and Chairman of UKERNA Ltd, the company that manages JANET, the UK's academic and research network. His main research interests are failure in complex human systems and change in higher education systems. He has edited and authored books on system failures, systems behaviour, corporate universities and the works of Sir Geoffrey Vickers.

PREFACE

Organizations need to process a rapidly growing amount of information and as individuals we rely on information systems for almost everything from health care and banking to our weekly shop at the supermarket. Yet at the same time as reliance on them grows, information systems continue to be particularly prone to failure. Some systems never materialize, others appear late and/or over budget and those that are implemented often fail to deliver the promised levels of performance. Worse still, developers and users experience the same types of problems again and again, despite the publicity given to those systems that have failed spectacularly at enormous cost.

There could be a variety of reasons for this absence of learning, but we are convinced that one is a culture of blame and another is the absence of robust methods for discovering anything other than the most superficial lessons. With this book we want to change both. We want to raise the status of the study of failures to a point where executive sponsors, politicians, administrators, analysts, developers, users and the like are proud to talk of the lessons they have learnt from the analysis of their own failures and those of others. We hope to encourage that by providing a highly developed and well-tested approach to the analysis of failures. By bringing complexity and interconnectivity to the surface we think we can provide a common language in which others can share experiences and benefit by learning from failure.

There are very many definitions of information systems. Some, such as the following example, emphasize the use of information and communication technology (ICT):

> Any telecommunications and/or computer related equipment or intercon-nected system or subsystems of equipment that is used in the acquisition, storage, manipulation, management, movement, control, display, switching, interchange, transmission, or reception of voice and/or data, and includes software, firmware, and hardware.
>
> *National Information Systems Security (INFOSEC) Glossary,*
> *NSTISSI No. 4009, January 1999 (Revision 1)*

Others narrow it down to systems that support management decision-making. This book adopts a broader view that goes well beyond the integration of hardware and software. It considers an information system to be any system that has collection, processing, dissemination and use of information as a major component in terms of its purpose and the activities it carries out. Most modern information systems with any degree of complexity will, in practice, almost always incorporate ICT, but the technology is not the defining aspect. The significant issues are the generation, processing and use of information.

We have enjoyed writing this book and hope that it will inspire you to join the growing band who are using these ideas in earnest. We look forward to hearing of your findings and experiences and incorporating them into subsequent editions.

ACKNOWLEDGEMENTS

We owe most thanks to our colleagues, especially Open University academics whether they be research students, professors or the associate lecturers who are the mainstay of the OU courses on which we have worked. Special mention must also go to the thousands of OU students we have had the pleasure of teaching.

We should also like to thank the many people who have given us specific help with this book. In particular, thanks are due to Diana White, Visiting Research Fellow at the OU, who has collaborated with us on research and undertaken some of the analysis presented here. We should also like to acknowledge Bill Dodd with whom we enjoyed working on the EPR project and thank the Information Management Group of the National Health Service Executive for permission to publish our study. Thanks go too to the National Audit Office both for their continued commitment to publishing their investigations of the public sector and their agreement to our use of material.

Thanks are also due to Diane Taylor at Wiley who encouraged us to write an earlier book, *Learning from Failure: The Systems Approach*, and to Sarah Booth and Rachel Goodyear who have been so helpful with this one.

Chapter 1

OPPORTUNITIES FOR LEARNING

Introduction

Millions of pounds are wasted on information system projects that fail and millions more are lost due to malfunctions of systems that have progressed beyond the implementation stage. The horror stories are easy to find, at least where large projects in the public sector are concerned. For example:

- In 1996 the Integrated Justice Project was set up in Ontario, Canada, with the aim of building an information system for Ontario's entire justice sector. In March 1998 the investment required was estimated to be $180 million and the benefits as $326 million. By March 2001 the figures had become an investment of $312 (of which $159 million had already been spent) and benefits of $238. Thus the benefit–investment ratio had changed from 1.81 : 1 to 0.76 : 1.
- Also in 1996 the Benefits Agency of the UK government's Department of Social Security and Post Office Counters Ltd awarded a contract to Pathway, a subsidiary of the ICL computer services group, to provide recipients of social security benefits with magnetic stripe payment cards. The project was abandoned exactly three years later. The National Audit Office estimated that the cancellation cost over £1 billion.
- In 1998 The Lord Chancellor's Department commissioned 'Libra', a system to support the work of magistrates' courts in England and Wales. By 2002 the cost of the project had doubled to almost £400 million but the scope had reduced drastically.
- In 1999 delays in processing British passport applications, following the introduction of the Passport Agency's new system, cost £12 million including, it is alleged, £16 000 spent on umbrellas to shelter those queuing in the rain to collect their passports.
- In 2002 a project to replace the British Army, Royal Navy and Royal Air Force inventory systems with a single system (the Defence Stores Management Solution) was brought to a halt after £130 million had been spent. Hardware worth a little over £12 million was able to be used elsewhere but the remaining £118 million was written off as a loss.

- In 2003 it was revealed that the British government had to pay over £2 million extra to its contractor, Capita, following a big increase in the number of applications for criminal records checks being made in writing instead of by telephone or electronically. This was just one of a series of adverse reports involving the Criminal Records Bureau. Some schools had to delay the start of the autumn term due to backlogs in the processing of teachers' applications, and at the start of November inquiries into the background of care workers in charge of children and the elderly were suspended for a period of up to 21 months in order to ease the pressure on the system.

Not all failures can be expressed in financial terms. On 19 January 1982, following the Byford Report on an inquiry into what had gone wrong with West Yorkshire Police's hunt for the serial killer dubbed 'The Yorkshire Ripper', the then Secretary of State for the Home Department, William Whitelaw, said to the House of Commons:

> Another serious handicap to the investigation was the ineffectiveness of the major incident room which became overloaded with unprocessed information. With hindsight, it is now clear that if these errors and inefficiencies had not occurred, Sutcliffe would have been identified as a prime suspect sooner than he was.

There seems to be widespread agreement that this identification could have occurred at least a full 18 months sooner. In those 18 months, another three women were murdered.

By 2004 police forces were still experiencing information system failures. A Public Inquiry report on child protection procedures in Humberside Police and Cambridgeshire Constabulary (Bichard, 2004) found:

> The process of creating records on their [Humberside Police's] main local intelligence system – called CIS Nominals – was fundamentally flawed ... Police Officers at various levels were alarmingly ignorant of how records were created and how the system worked. The guidance and training available were inadequate and this fed the confusion which surrounded the review and deletion of records once they had been created.

> The failures in the use of CIS Nominals were compounded by the fact that other systems were also not being operated properly. Information was not recorded correctly onto the separate CIS Crime system. It took four years

(from 1999 to 2003) for those carrying out vetting checks to be told that the
CIS 2 system, introduced in late 1999, also allowed them to check a name
through the CIS Crime system.

(Bichard, 2004, p. 2)

The private sector also has its share of failures, although they tend to be smaller in
scale and are often hidden behind closed doors. Nevertheless, examples do emerge into
the public gaze:

- On 25 February 2000 at the High Court, Queens Bench Division, Technology and
  Construction Court, Wang (UK) Limited was ordered to pay damages of a little over
  £9 million to Pegler Ltd, a Doncaster-based engineering firm. Wang had entered
  into a contract to supply Pegler with a bespoke computer system to process sales,
  despatch, accounts and manufacturing systems and associated project management
  and consultancy services. Six years after the contract was signed it was formally
  terminated by Pegler but, in effect, it had been abandoned by Wang before that.
  Wang claimed that exclusion causes in the contract meant that it was not liable
  for damages, but the court found against it and it had to pay compensation for
  lost opportunities, wasted management time and reduced business efficiency and
  recompense Pegler for money it had spent elsewhere on outsourcing and software
  acquisition.
- In 2002 in the USA, the pharmaceutical company Eli Lilly settled out of court
  with the Federal Trade Commission after being accused of violating its own online
  privacy policy by revealing the e-mail addresses of 669 patients who were taking the
  antidepressant drug, Prozac.
- Also in 2002 the Dutch Quest division of ICI, which makes fragrances for perfume
  manufacturers, lost an estimated £14 million as a result of problems with its new
  SAP enterprise resource management system.
- At the start of 2003, the first stage of a legal battle to recover £11 million was
  fought by the Co-operative Group against Fujitsu Services (formerly ICL). The
  case concerned alleged shortcomings in a programme to install a common IT
  infrastructure across the whole of the Co-operative Group following the merger
  between the Co-operative Wholesale Society (CWS) and the Co-operative Retail
  Services (CRS). A significant aspect of the problem was the system needed to spread
  CWS's dividend loyalty card across all the Group's stores.
- In May 2003, Energywatch, the independent gas and electricity consumer watchdog
  set up by the Utilities Act (2000), published information claiming that billing

problems had affected 500 000 gas and electricity consumers over the previous 12 months. Research conducted on their behalf by NOP World suggested that 9% of consumers had experienced debt due to estimated billing. The cost to consumers was stated to be £2 million in avoidable debt. It was also estimated that almost 50 000 British Gas customers throughout the UK do not receive their first bill for up to a year and, as a consequence, owe British Gas around £13 million. In 1999 British Gas served a writ on systems supplier SCT International claiming damages in respect of software it had supplied for billing business gas customers.

Examples such as these lie at or near the pinnacle of a mountain of failure. Beneath lies examples such as the incident in Japan on 1 March 2003 when failure of the system that transmits such data as flight numbers and flight plans to airports led to the cancellation of 122 flights and delays to a further 721. On the lowest slopes are the failures we all experience on a regular basis such as the long queue at the library while the numbers of the borrowers and their books are written out by hand because the system is down again and the delay at the supermarket checkout because a price is missing on the point of sale system. Obviously, not every coding error or design snag or glitch in the operation of an information system merits serious investigation, but even when these failures are excluded there are still ample left to study.

Opportunity for learning

In wondering what can be done about such failures, two things are indisputable: first, some failures will always occur and, second, the vast majority are avoidable. The reasons why they are not avoided are manifold, but a major reason is the inability to learn from mistakes. A survey by Ewusi-Mensah and Przasnyski (1995) provides one explanation of this lack of learning. In an attempt to discover the kind of post-mortem appraisals that had been carried out, they conducted a survey of companies that had abandoned information system (IS) development projects. Their findings suggested 'that most organizations do not keep records of their failed projects and do not make any formal efforts to understand what went wrong or attempt to learn from their failed projects' (p. 3).

Emergency planning has tended to be the norm in many high-risk technologies, such as nuclear power generation and oil production, and the number of commercial organizations making similar plans is increasing, especially since the attacks on the World Trade Center in New York in 2001. However, there are still a significant number who seem to be remarkably reluctant to anticipate that things might go wrong with their information systems. A Global Information Security Survey of 1400 organizations in 66 countries conducted by Ernst & Young in 2003 found that over 34% of those surveyed felt themselves to be 'less than adequate' at determining whether or not their systems were currently under attack, and over 33% felt that they were 'inadequate' in their ability to respond to incidents. A similar survey of the world's biggest companies, conducted by market analyst Meta Research in the same year, found that only 60% had 'a credible disaster recovery plan that is up-to-date, tested and executable'. The picture is unlikely to be rosier where smaller organizations are concerned.

One of the features of information systems that renders them prone to failure is the very high extent to which they need to be embedded in the organizations using them. As Walsham (1993, p. 223) says:

> The technical implementation of computer-based IS is clearly necessary, but is not sufficient to ensure organizational implementation with respect to such aspects as high levels of organizational use or positive perceptions by stakeholder groups. Organizational implementation involves a *process of social change* over the whole time extending from the system's initial conceptualization through to technical implementation and the post-implementation period.

Given this need to take account of the organizational setting of an IS, learning at the level of the organization is likely to be particularly important.

Organizational learning

Argyris and Schon, the founding fathers of the concept of organizational learning, began their first major book on the topic with a story about failure:

> Several years ago the top management of a multibillion dollar corporation decided that Product X was a failure and should be disbanded. The losses involved exceeded one hundred million dollars. At least five people knew that Product X was a failure six years before the decision was taken to stop producing it. . . .

> (Argyris & Schon, 1978, p. 1)

They then examined why production had continued for so long, and concluded:

> Difficulties with and barriers to organizational learning arose as it became clear that the original decision (and hence the planning and problem solving that led to the decision) was wrong. Questioning the original decision violated a set of nested organizational norms. The first norm was that policies and objectives, especially those that top management was excited about, should not be confronted openly. The second norm was that bad news in memos to the top had to be offset by good news. (p. 3)

Similar scenarios, where organizations continue with a system that is not delivering, are by no means rare in the information system domain.

The main thrust of Argyris and Schon's argument is that organizational learning involves the detection and correction of error. They draw a distinction between two types of learning: single loop and double loop.

> When the error detected and corrected permits the organization to carry on its present policies or achieve its present objectives, then that error-detection-and-correction process is *single-loop* learning. Single-loop learning is like a thermostat that learns when it is too hot or too cold and turns the heat on or off. The thermostat can perform this task because it can receive information (the temperature of the room) and take corrective action. *Double-loop* learning occurs when error is detected and corrected in ways that involve the modification of an organization's underlying norms, policies, and objectives. (pp. 2–3)

They emphasize that both types of learning are required by all organizations, and in a later work Argyris (1992, p. 9) provides guidance on the use of each:

> Single-loop learning is appropriate for the routine, repetitive issue – it helps to get the everyday job done. Double-loop learning is more relevant for the complex non-programmable issues – it assures that there will be another day in the future of the organization.

It is Argyris and Schon's assertion that 'organizations tend to create learning systems that inhibit double-loop learning' (p. 4).

The work of Argyris and Schon emphasizes the learning process. Senge (1990) gives it a stronger practical focus by identifying the following five disciplines, or bodies of theory and technique, which, when brought together, create the capacity to learn:

1. *Systems thinking* – which integrates the other four disciplines. For Senge this is concerned with seeing developing patterns rather than snapshots. 'At the heart of the learning organization is a shift of mind – from seeing ourselves as separate from the world to being connected to the world, from seeing problems caused by someone or something "out there" to seeing how our own actions create the problems we experience.'
2. *Personal mastery* – a personal commitment to lifelong learning by individuals in the organization. Mastery is seen in the craft sense of constantly striving to improve on the personal skills that the individual has acquired.
3. *Mental models* – Senge argues that there are deeply ingrained assumptions and images that influence both the way individuals perceive the world and the actions that are taken. These mental models are different from the 'espoused theories' in that they are based on observed behaviour. In Senge's view, these models need to be brought into the open so that they can be subjected to scrutiny.
4. *Building shared vision* – Senge posits that if organizations are to be successful everyone must pull in the same direction towards the same vision of the future – and they must do that because they want to, not because they are told to. 'You don't get people to buy into a vision, you get them to enrol.' The commitment to learning is a part of that vision.
5. *Team learning* – the team rather than the individual is the key learning unit in most views of a learning organization. Primarily this is because a team is regarded as a microcosm of a whole organization, but it may also be influenced by the knowledge that there was already a body of established management literature on the creation of successful teams.

As can be seen from the above, much of the thrust of Senge's approach is linked to the idea of human-centred management; it is about allowing the individuals throughout an organization to contribute fully to its future development, and about making sure that senior management discharge their responsibilities for ensuring that strategy is clearly articulated and that staff are nurtured.

In a paper published in 1991, Huber sets out four constructs that he regards as integrally linked to organizational learning. These are: knowledge acquisition; information distribution; information interpretation; and decision-making. Argyris and Schon's work has been criticized (see Sun & Scott, 2003, p. 205) for not addressing 'the triggers that spur the learning process'. In his unpicking of knowledge acquisition, Huber goes some way towards addressing this. He identifies five processes through which organizations can obtain knowledge:

1. *Congenital learning* This involves taking on board the knowledge inherited at the conception of the organization and the additional knowledge acquired prior to its birth.
2. *Experiential learning* This can be achieved in a number of ways and can even be unintentional.
3. *Vicarious learning* This is the acquisition of second-hand experience from other, often competing, organizations and is often accomplished by imitation.
4. *Grafting* Knowledge is acquired by recruiting new members with the desired knowledge, sometimes to the extent of taking over a complete organization.
5. *Searching and noticing* This can take three forms: scanning the environment; focused search; and monitoring of the organization's performance.

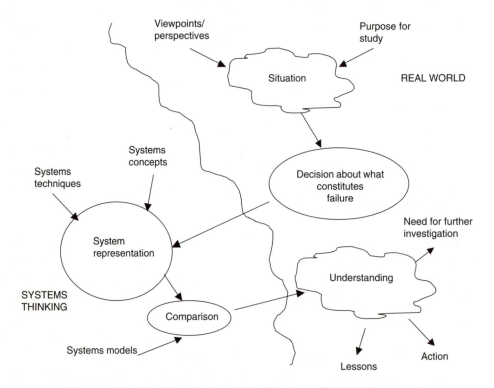

Figure 1.1 A notional view of the Systems Failures Approach

However, as Sun and Scott (2003, pp. 206–207) point out, both Huber and Senge concentrate on explicit knowledge and thereby fail to consider tacit knowledge to a sufficient extent. One of the advantages of the Systems Failures Approach is that it can develop tacit knowledge to the point where it can be replicated. As with other systems approaches, such as Soft Systems Analysis (SSA) and Total Systems Intervention (TSI), the Systems Failures Approach takes the analyst from the real world (in this case the situation labelled as a failure or a potential failure) into the conceptual world where systems thinking, qualitative modelling and comparison provide the means by which understanding can be achieved. This understanding is then taken back to the real world, where it emerges as a set of lessons that can be shared. This journey is illustrated in Figure 1.1.

Beyond the organization

Although they sometimes appear startlingly reluctant to do so, organizations can also learn from one another, and in the field of IS development it is very important that they should do so, even where a single organization might only undertake a large project once in a blue moon.

A major source of lessons that is widely available is in public administration and governance. In the UK a long series of high-profile and very costly failures led the Committee on Public Accounts to investigate 'more than 25 cases from the 1990s where the implementation of IT systems has resulted in delay, confusion and inconvenience to the citizen and, in many cases, poor value for money to the taxpayer' (Committee of Public Accounts, 1999). Every one of the cases they looked at was an IS project. As a result of this investigation, and additional criticism from the National Audit Office, a major review of government IT projects was commissioned by the Prime Minister. Its findings were published by the Cabinet Office in May 2000 in a report (Cabinet Office, 2000) that sets out measures to improve project delivery and includes 30 recommendations that aim to ensure that all government IT projects are as good as the best.

Before leaving the topic of learning from one another, it is worth asking the question: 'Are IS failures different from other failures?' This book deals specifically with information system failures but the Systems Failures Approach is equally applicable to all sorts of complex failure situations from natural disasters, transport accidents, construction projects, company collapses, large-scale frauds, etc. Although it is debatable whether IS failures are different, they certainly have many features in common with those experienced elsewhere, as you will see in the following chapter where we look at the characteristics of failure.

Overview of the book

The aim of this book is to promote learning by providing a general understanding of the nature of failure and a systems approach (the Systems Failures Approach) by which it can be analysed, understood and predicted. The main argument is that through the use of systems thinking it is possible to gain insights into failure that would not otherwise be available. The book also introduces a variety of methods and techniques that have been developed by others, and thus allows the reader to see them alongside the Systems Failures Approach put forward by the authors. The emphasis here is on taking learning beyond direct personal experience to a level that encompasses learning from situations in which one played no part, and of which one might have had no direct experience.

Chapter 2 looks at the nature of success and failure and at ways in which IS failures can be classified. It explores the stages of the IS life cycle to identify points where things may go awry.

Chapter 3 tells the story of two projects. At the outset the projects seemed to be very similar and equally likely to succeed. They were about the same size and scope and the organizations in which they were being undertaken had many features in common. In the event, however, the two projects could not have been more different in one extremely important respect: one was largely successful across the whole of the range of measures normally used to judge success; but the other exhibited most of the characteristics of failure.

Chapter 4 introduces a range of systems concepts and shows how their use can lead to an understanding of a failure situation. Among the concepts covered are: appreciative system, holism, environment, boundary, hierarchy, control and communication.

Chapter 5 is another case study. It is based on two reports commissioned by Cambridge University into the development of an online commitment accounting software system. The project attracted widespread bad publicity for the University with headlines pointing to the waste of £10 million. Worse still, the system continued to cause disruption to the University's activities long after it was installed, and led to calls to examine the way the University is governed. This case, together with those in

Chapter 3, provides examples for Chapters 6 and 7, which look at how the Systems Failures Approach works. It also provides source material with which others can conduct their own analyses.

Chapters 8 and 9 are also built around case studies. Chapter 8 looks at two of the examples mentioned at the beginning of the chapter: the Benefits Payment Card project that was abandoned after three years, and Project Libra, the magistrates' court information system. In Chapter 9 the direction of the analysis changes from looking backwards to looking forwards. The main purpose of Chapter 9 is to illustrate the process of using the Systems Failures Approach to prevent failure. It reports a study that was commissioned by the Department of Health as it embarked upon a large-scale IS project to design, develop and implement electronic patient records. The study was in two parts: first, published accounts (mainly American and Canadian) of attempts to introduce clinical information systems were analysed; then the findings of the first stage, together with lessons from other large-scale IS projects and information gained from interviews with interested parties, were used to look forward to the development and introduction of the National Health Service's new system with a view to predicting the system's associated risks.

Chapter 10 examines various approaches that different authors have taken to understand, explain, intervene in and prevent failures. The chapter begins with project management approaches relevant to IS failures. It then moves on to discuss general approaches to failure and specific approaches developed to understand IS failures. It ends by returning to the Systems Failures Approach.

Throughout this book the emphasis will tend to be on practical application, with the theory that underpins the work being brought in to explain what is being undertaken, and why. Case studies are used as the vehicle for introducing the Systems Failures Approach and for demonstrating it in action, with further case study material being supplied to enable the reader to try out the ideas, techniques and procedures.

References

Argyris, C. (1992) *On Organizational Learning*. Blackwell, Oxford.

Argyris, C. & Schon, D.A. (1978) *Organizational Learning: A Theory of Action Perspective*. Addison-Wesley, Reading, MA.

Bichard, M. (2004) *The Bichard Inquiry Report*. The Stationery Office, London.

Cabinet Office (2000) *Successful IT: Modernising Government in Action*. Cabinet Office.

Committee of Public Accounts (1999) *Improving the Delivery of Government IT Projects*. Committee of Public Accounts.

Ernst & Young (2003) *Global Information Security Survey*. Ernst & Young.

Ewusi-Mensah, K. & Przasnyski, Z.H. (1995) Learning from abandoned information development projects. *Journal of Information Technology*, 10: 3–14.

Huber, G.P. (1991) Organizational learning: The contributing processes and the literatures. *Organization Science*, 2: 88–115.

Senge, P.M. (1990) The leader's new work: Building learning organizations. *Sloan Management Review*, 7–23.

Sun, P.Y.T. & Scott, J.L. (2003) Exploring the divide – organizational learning and learning organization. *The Learning Organization*, 10: 202–215.

Walsham, G. (1993) *Interpreting Information Systems in Organizations*. John Wiley & Sons, Chichester.

Chapter 2

WHAT IS AN INFORMATION SYSTEM FAILURE?

Introduction

As information systems are complex and multifaceted, failure (and success) can be manifested in many ways. Chapter 1 presented examples of information systems that have reputedly failed in one way or another; have cost more than originally planned; have never worked as they were intended; or have disappointed in some way or another.

This chapter interrogates the notion of IS failures and explores the stages of the IS life cycle to identify points at which things may go awry. The development of the ideas of failure and life cycle will provide a foundation for the more comprehensive analysis of failure later in the book.

A definition of success

A closer examination of even a few examples of situations in which failure is said to have occurred, such as those cited in Chapter 1, leads to a simple definition of what something that is not a failure, i.e. a success, might look like.

> *The system achieved what was intended of it; it was operational at the time and cost that were planned; the project team and the users are pleased with the result and they continue to be satisfied afterwards.*

This commonsense definition is not far from a systematic study (Wateridge, 1997) that identified six important ways in which *success* could be measured: meeting user requirements, achieving its purposes, meeting timescales and budgets, making the users happy, and meeting quality standards.

However, if we take the view that an IS has failed if it misses any of the criteria that are implicit in the above definition of success, then it is hardly surprising that some observers have argued that most large and many small IS projects are failures. For example, Sauer (1988) comments:

> Some systems never work. The full suite of programs and files are never made operational because they will be unacceptable to the user. Some work, but come in either cripplingly over budget, very late, or both. Others are pared down in terms of facilities, while still others are literally forced into place in their host organisation, despite their being either inappropriate or unacceptable. Some perform to specification but turn out to be so inflexible that maintenance and enhancement assume nightmarish proportions. Others are thought to work, but turn out not to.

Certainly, the judgement about whether a particular IS is classified as a failure or a success will often be contested. The disputes may involve the internal politics of an organization and, at times, they may be legal and contractual or even academic. To learn lessons from these 'failures' first requires an understanding of these differences of view.

Starting to disentangle the above definition of success highlights some of the difficulties encountered when considering success or failure.

- *The system achieved what was intended*

  Implicit in this part of the definition is the idea that the system is clear and known, there were stated and agreed objectives for an IS development and that it is possible to measure performance of the IS against these objectives.

- *... it was operational at the time and cost that were planned*

  Here the embedded concepts are: (1) that there was an agreed and approved development plan that included costs and timescales and has stayed the same throughout the project; (2) that performance against this plan can be measured; and (3) that satisfactory operational performance can be identified and agreed.

- *... the project team and the users are pleased with the result*

  There are a number of potentially conflicting ideas here too. First, there is the relative viewpoint and importance of users and developers. It might seem to some that the views of the project team are paramount. After all, they are the professionals who were charged with the responsibility for producing the system. Indeed some have suggested that their judgement is the only one that matters and success should be judged by them. However, others might see the team as largely irrelevant as long as the users are content. But who are the users? Are they the same as the client or customer? Are the users just the people who interact directly with the system or do they include those who may not know it exists but are users of the services it supports?

- ... *and they continue to be satisfied afterwards.*

There are several nuances in this aspect of the definition too. First, *whose* degree of satisfaction is to be considered later? They may not be the original users, however defined. Secondly, when is this *later satisfaction* to be ascertained and against what criteria? The IS may be judged against a different set of standards than those originally envisaged. In other words, the environment may have changed so that the IS is now expected to do things that were not envisaged when the original system was designed. Indeed, an innovation may have been so successful that users and others can only later see what more could have been achieved.

A simple framework for examining the success of an information system project involves asking the questions posed in Table 2.1.

Table 2.1 Framework for examining success	
Was the project:	Completed?
	Well managed?
	Within budget/schedule?
	Used/supported?
Did the project:	Meet its objectives (client requirements/organizational objectives)?
	Perform as intended/is technically sound/is appropriate?
	(Not) Display undesirable side effects?
	Meet quality/safety standards?
	Fit in/adapt to its environment?
	Provide intended/required business/other benefits?
	Fit in with rest of the organization/cause minimal business disruption?
	Provide long-term benefits?

Failures

One approach to understanding the complexity and ambiguity that surrounds notions of success and failure is to absorb the idea that judgement about success and failure is subjective and depends upon the standpoint of the observer(s). For example, Lyytinen and Hirschheim (1987) view IS failures as expectation failures. They identify the stakeholders – i.e. the people inside and outside an organization who have a vested interest in a situation, such as the client, customers and users (after Mason & Mitroff, 1981) – and then they map the problems that those stakeholders perceive.

There are similarities between this treatment and earlier work on failures in a wider context than information systems. Naughton and Peters (1976) referred to the failures arising from sets of related activities as Systems Failures and characterized them as relying on:

- human perception and identification as a failure, thereby acknowledging that one person's failure may be another person's success; and either:
- failure to meet system objectives attributed by those involved, such as designers and users; or
- the production of outputs that are considered to be undesirable by those involved.

This definition was endorsed by Vickers (1981) who simplified part of it as: 'A human system fails if it does not succeed in doing what it was designed to do; or if it succeeds but leaves everyone wishing it had never tried.'

It is the rather wide definition of systems failures, where significance is in the eye of the beholder, that has been the basis of much of the research work referred to in this book. However, these broad definitions are not without their critics. Sauer (1993), for example, criticizes the plurality of Lyytinen and Hirschheim's model and, by implication, the Systems Failures definition. His view is that 'an information system should only be deemed a failure when development or operation ceases, leaving supporters dissatisfied with the extent to which the system has served their interests'.

The Systems Failures definition contains within it an additional and important point about the undesirable or unexpected consequences of an IS development. These type-2 failures (Fortune & Peters, 1995) occur when the original objectives may be met but there are also consequences or side-effects that are judged to be inappropriate or undesirable. Thus, in the world of IS, a type-2 failure might be a suite of programs that work well, but leave the company vulnerable because they create a security loophole or a dependency on a third party. Perversely, a type-2 failure could result from too much success. For example, a New Zealand financial services company engaged in a whole-hearted re-engineering of the accountancy functions in its head office and its nine regional subsidiaries. The carefully designed project was implemented to schedule with the systems going on-line on 1 December; surplus staff were made redundant in January as the accountancy staff were reduced from 75 to 24; and the project was finally signed off and handed over early in March. However, by April an Australian-owned financial services company announced that it was buying 100% of the New Zealand company. The success of the IS and the associated business re-engineering had made the company much more attractive as a potential acquisition (Larsen & Myers, 1999).

These type-2 failures, and the more obvious type-1 failures (where the objectives of the designers, sponsors, or users are not met fully), are not mutually exclusive; an object may fail to live up to expectations and still have undesirable consequences.

Failures in information system projects

Information systems and information technology projects are frequently expensive and increasingly are high risk. As organizations rely more heavily on information and computerized transactions in a rapidly changing technological environment, they are faced progressively with new software systems and changes in hardware which, if introduced unsuccessfully, may mean that the organization can no longer transact its business. In June 2004, the Royal Bank of Canada (RBC) had a week in which it could not tell its 10 million customers with any certainty how much was in their accounts, and RBC and other banks' customer accounts were not being credited with items such as salary payments (Saunders & Bloom, 2004). Once the fault was corrected the bank not only issued a public apology but had to reimburse its customers for banking service charges, fees and overdraft interest incurred, as well as reimburse other financial institutions for charges they had to refund to their customers.

In fact, the RBC changes were not a project but part of the ongoing improvement programme that information systems require. However, new organizations and start-up ventures increasingly rely upon technology, and that makes them particularly vulnerable to shortcomings in information systems. One example is the decision by the Higher Education Funding Council for England to invest over £60 million in the creation of an organization called UK e-Universities Worldwide Ltd. The aim was to market internationally e-learning courses created by universities. An early decision was taken that an essential element of the activity would be a purpose-built e-learning platform to be co-developed with an industrial partner. The development of an effective platform became a central focus of the organization. The platform was late in providing the functionality and performance that had been envisaged by many users. By early 2004 the decision was taken to cease international activity. Recruitment had been disappointing, but the absence of a fully effective e-learning platform left the company with little prospect of an alternative business stream (MacLeod, 2004). Over the next few months, small 'public good' activities that were being managed by the company were hived off to other organizations, and in mid-2004 the company was wound up.

UK e-Universities Worldwide Ltd was a start-up company and one cause of its demise was due to the delays and lack of functionality of the information systems (in this case called an e-learning platform) that were being built for it. The construction of the e-learning platform was a project. Compared with an ongoing activity, it should be relatively easy to decide what constitutes failure and success where a project is concerned. In theory at least, a project is capable of specification, and the objectives for what it is supposed to achieve can be, and normally are, formalized and later refined. So success and failure can be couched in terms of whether a project met its technical objectives, and how successfully it was managed. Fortune (1987) identified the three main threats to project success as cost escalation, delay and client dissatisfaction with the outcome. Pinto and Mantel (1990) also suggest that there are three distinct aspects of project performance against which success or failure can be assessed:

- The *implementation process*, where they see the key issue as efficiency measured in terms of criteria such as on schedule, to budget, meeting technical goals, and so on.
- The *value and usefulness* of the project as perceived by the project team – in effect, this is the project team's judgement about how professional a job they did.
- Finally, the *client satisfaction* with the project as delivered.

A project may not meet expectations on any one or a combination of these three aspects, and so the ambiguity about the extent and nature of failure persists in projects too. Mansell (1993), for example, describes a failures study of an information technology project. The project, which 'had become legendary in the company as a failure in the application of information technology', was late and over budget, but on the other hand there was no loss of service to the users. So this project failed on two counts out of three. In this particular case Mansell also reports the existence of type-2 failures: the 'other adverse effects of this project were a loss of staff morale and user confidence'. Though even on this score, judgement about success and failure depend upon the criteria being used to measure the performance, since he also reports that 'Staff who left the company had no difficulty in gaining alternative employment'.

The embedded nature of an IS

One of the difficulties in judging the performance of information systems arises from the context in which they exist. Even though many organizations are dependent upon their IT and IS, the organization and the technology are not synonymous. So it is a rare occurrence when a new set of hardware or software is introduced without there being a set of other associated changes within the organization. More commonly, when a set of business processes is being redesigned, the alterations in the information systems are an essential element of the change.

For example, when the MIT set out on a 'Re-engineering Project' to redesign parts of its administrative activities around a set of information systems, the project started with grand intentions but, like so many before and since, it became synonymous with the introduction of a specific computer system. In the course of this long project, the embedded nature of the IS became very apparent. Even a deceptively simple stage such as the introduction of computerized class lists required significant changes in MIT policy and practice since it transpired that there was no agreed definition of who was a student of a particular class, and nor was it clear how students were admitted (Peters, 2003; Williams, 2002).

In a commercial context, the business case for investment in the (re)development of the computer systems will usually depend upon the potential for increased efficiency in the organization, and often the improved performance, increased revenues or reduced costs will be found in departments other than the one responsible for the IS developments.

In the minds of many participants, an IS development can be so linked with a set of organizational changes that the same name is used for both. Not surprisingly, they define 'the system' in different ways and, needless to say, have quite different criteria for judging success. (Defining 'the system' to be considered is an important element of the approach that will be described later in the book.) So, for example, within an organization, the finance director, the head of human resources, the IS project manager and the users will see an IS development very differently. When there is also ambiguity about whether the items being judged are the changes resulting from a new IS, or the changes resulting from the associated re-engineering, the differences of view are even more pronounced.

Information systems are often large and high-profile investments, but they are not alone either in being seen to be problematic or in being hard to judge in terms of their performance. In the 1960s Operations Research, or Operational Research as it is known in the UK, had a high profile in improving business efficiency. Yet in one of the classic pieces of evidence a leading OR figure, West Churchman, surveyed the first six years of the *Journal of the Operations Research Society of America*, but did not find a single example where there was sufficient evidence to indicate that the findings had been implemented (Churchman, 1964). Subsequent studies came to more optimistic conclusions, but some showed once again the subjective nature of the judgement about success and failure. An example in Figure 2.1 shows the results of a survey conducted by Wedley and Ferrie (1978) of 49 OR/management science projects and how their success was judged by the analysts and the managers responsible for their implementation. Whereas the analysts viewed 63% of the projects as successful and implemented, the managers placed only 20% in this category.

Nor are issues of success and failure clear cut in other organizational settings; indeed, there is an entire literature on defining organizational failure (cf. Mellahi & Wilkinson, 2004). Even something as apparently clear-cut as a company going into liquidation will not be viewed as a failure if, for example, the company was set up to handle risks on

		Analysts' classification		
		Unsuccessful	Successful but unimplemented	Successful and implemented
	Unsuccessful	6%	6%	10%
Managers' classification	Successful but unimplemented	10%	14%	33%
	Successful and implemented	0%	0%	20%

Figure 2.1 Distribution of projects by implementation status as classified by analysts and managers

behalf of partners or the parent company. In some cases such a company may act like a fuse in an electrical system and be designed to fail in certain circumstances. (These are classified as type-3 failures in Fortune and Peters, 1995.)

Information system life cycles

A development project for an information system could fail at a number of stages, from its initial conception through to its implementation and subsequent maintenance. Therefore, in trying to analyse and understand an IS failure it can be helpful to consider the many stages of an IS development. One common description of the stages of an information system project is known as the systems development life cycle (SDLC).

Although there are many variants, the SDLC has the following basic structure (after Avison & Fitzgerald, 2003):

- feasibility study
- systems investigation
- systems analysis
- systems design
- implementation
- review and maintenance.

The feasibility study looks at current arrangements and the needs the new system will have to meet and puts forward a series of potential solutions. The feasibility of each option is examined and an outline functional specification is drawn up for the most promising solution. The systems investigation gathers more detailed information about requirements, constraints, and the like. Systems analysis is a precursor to design and puts yet more flesh on the 'requirements' bones as well as investigating current structures and processes further. The systems design stage looks at all parts of the proposed new system and specifies them more precisely in terms of inputs, data capture methods, outputs, transformation processes, file structure and security and back-up mechanisms. Plans to test and implement the system are also developed at this stage.

The implementation stage involves sourcing the new system, writing and testing software, training users and testing aspects of the system as they become operational. Documentation is also prepared and security and back-up procedures are also tested.

The stage usually ends at the point where acceptance testing has been completed and the new system is deemed to be fully operational. Review and maintenance is the name given to those processes designed to ensure that the system continues to perform well.

The SDLC stages provide one framework for looking at the phases of an IS development and hence the opportunity for failure at each one. It is not completely comprehensive for two reasons. First, it could be argued that failures can occur before the feasibility stage at the point where a need has been identified but steps to fill it have not progressed sufficiently far to reach the start of a feasibility study. Evidence for pre-feasibility failure might be the lack of a mechanism to meet genuine information needs in a timely and effective manner. However, finding evidence of something that did not really get started is intrinsically difficult, and the belief that there was a need that warranted a feasibility study will be particularly subjective. Indeed, in some circumstances knowledgeable participants may believe that the failure to embark upon the first stage of the SDLC can rightly be regarded as a success.

Much more importantly, the descriptions of SDLC, and many other variations on IS development, are concerned with a relatively narrow view of IS processes, as seen from the standpoint of the IS developer. However, a few of these descriptions are much more explicit about seeing the IS as simply a part of a much wider business context. One generic example is the work system life cycle (WSLC) model (Alter, 2001), which has the following stages:

- Initiation
- Development
- Implementation
- Operation and Maintenance.

The stages of the WSLC may look similar to the SDLC, but what makes them different is that the former recognizes the wider organizational activity within which the software and the hardware are components. Alter sees an organization as made up of a set of work systems, such as systems to procure materials from suppliers, or create financial reports, or coordinate work across departments. A work system is defined as a system in which human participants and/or machines perform a business process using information, technology and other resources to produce products and/or services for internal or external customers.

There are a number of distinctive features of this approach. First, such phrases as implementation, operation and maintenance can have a different and much broader meaning when they refer to the work system rather than the information system. There is no longer any possibility that they simply refer to the technology and the software. Secondly, this is more obviously an iterative model than a linear process, as can be seen in Figure 2.2.

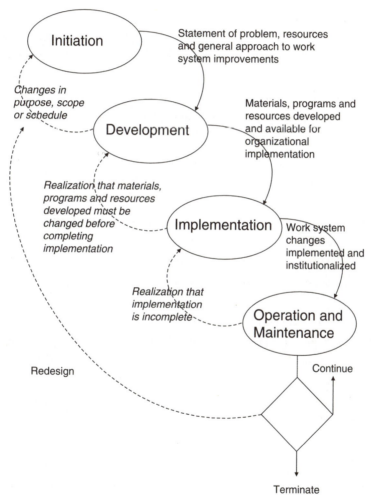

Figure 2.2 The work system life cycle (after Alter, 2001).
Based upon 'Which life cycle – work system, information system, or software?' by Alter, S. © 2001. Used with permission from Association for Information Systems, Atlanta, GA; 404-651-0348. All rights reserved.

The iterative nature of this model, and the emphasis it places upon implementation and operation, bring us to another important area of information systems. Some may be newly developed on a 'green-field' site but others have evolved over time.

Systems evolution

There are two important ways of looking at information systems that lead to different ways of considering their success or failure. In the straightforward case, which we have considered so far in this chapter, an information system can be considered as a project that is instigated, specified, designed and eventually implemented and maintained. It goes through a life cycle like the one described above. When big, high-profile information system projects fail, they attract significant amounts of publicity, especially if they are in the public sector, and their consequences are often dramatic and far-reaching.

At another extreme, there are information systems that form sets of subsystems that work together to deliver an overall IS. The subsystems may be modified and updated, new items may be introduced and redundant ones removed. People may talk about this being a single IS, and it may be criticized or deemed to be a failure, but neither it nor its predecessors need ever have been designed as a complete whole. Evolved information systems may develop slowly over a long period of time, sometimes changing imperceptibly and sometimes being the subject of fairly major modifications. Such systems can fail catastrophically, but it is often the case that they gradually become unable to cope with the demands placed upon them until, if not modified, they reach a point where they start to cause serious harm to the activities they were designed to support. David Slider, managing director, Europe, Middle East, Africa, at Fidelity Information Services – a major supplier to the banking industry (quoted in Imeson, 2003) – attests to the existence of such systems:

> When I walk into a bank, it's not uncommon to see systems 20, 30, 40 years old that have been patched up over time. They are not well documented and frequently include computer languages written by programmers who have nearly all retired. Soon there will be nobody left to re-code them.
>
> There are lots more banks with systems that are past their prime than there are with modern systems.

The Royal Bank of Canada may not fit this description since it had invested heavily in information technology, but the impact on the bank and its customers arose not from the introduction of a new IS but from a relatively small change to an existing program which, in turn, had potential implications for other systems within the bank.

Responding to symptoms of failure

The example of the Royal Bank of Canada shows how an information system does not exist in isolation and how relatively small technical problems can have serious implications. In this case, a relatively small programming change was introduced on the evening of Monday, 31 May 2004. By early on 1 June, the error had been identified and within two hours it had been corrected. However, the bank had partially completed its production run and it needed to ensure that the error did not pose a risk to other systems. The decision was therefore made to stop production. Once production was restarted, the verification processes took longer than expected because transactions for two consecutive days needed to be processed on the same date. This, in turn, required further manual verification of dates, adding to the backlog. In the circumstances, scheduling needed to be handled manually rather than automatically, and it was decided to give priority to payroll transactions. As a result of these two factors, the bank realized that it would not be able to be fully operational in time for normal opening on 4 June but would need the weekend to eliminate the backlog. On 7 June, it had managed to return to normal operations, but was still faced with the task of dealing with the consequential results for the individual accounts mentioned earlier. Banks and other organizations have contingency plans and procedures to deal with emergencies or unusual events, whether they are terrorist attacks, hardware failures or serious fraud, and RBC and other banks reviewed their procedures as a result of this event. However, large-scale IS developments raise a different set of issues and seem to possess a number of features that make them more difficult to manage. Certainly, their course seems to be harder to predict and manage than smaller projects or more mature technologies, such as construction engineering.

The Royal Academy of Engineering and The British Computer Society (2004) suggested that difficulties with IS management are due to features such as the lack of constraints in thinking about possible applications, the difficulty to visualizing the possibilities, complexity, and uncertainty surrounding requirements and implementation.

However, when an information system development is run as a project, then any of the many project management methods that are regularly used in IS development should show up slippages in budget expenditure or schedule, and usually they will also highlight design issues. Chapter 4 looks at the feedback and control mechanisms that can be deployed to assess progress, but what happens when information from the project monitoring shows that all is not going exactly to plan? Research evidence, as well as experience and anecdote, suggests that slippage is common, but the necessary corrective action is not always taken.

The extreme examples of things going awry are 'runaway projects' that continue to be delayed and consume resources and cannot apparently be brought under control. Keil, Mann and Rai (2000) have tested four theoretical approaches to try to explain how these projects escalate. *Self-justification theory* posits that managers continue with projects to justify, to themselves and others, their previous decisions. *Prospect theory* suggests that those involved continue to take risks with a project because they are faced with a certain failure or some (possibly low) probability of success albeit with a greater cost. *Agency theory* meanwhile highlights the imbalance in information between managers who oversee projects and their agents who have the technical expertise and detailed knowledge. And *approach avoidance theory* highlights the restraining factors that encourage avoidance being outweighed by the driving forces seeking continuance. The agency theory includes the notion that apparent nearness to completion is a force for continuing, but, with hindsight, projects are often reported as near to completion for some considerable time. Indeed, it is not unheard of for a project to be '90% complete' for half of the project's life. Keil, Mann and Rai (2000) surveyed IT auditors and found that all the theories were found to be significant, but the completion effect was reported in 70% of runaway projects.

Conclusion

Failure and success are subjective assessments that vary with time and the standpoint of the person making the judgement. In analysing an IS failure there is advantage in being aware of the life cycle of IS projects and work on failures in other domains. It is not helpful to view information systems without considering the environment in which they operate since, in many cases, the source and the manifestation of the failure may be outside the IS as specified originally.

References

Alter, S. (2001) Which life cycle – work system, information system, or software? *Communications of the Association for Information Systems*, 7: Article 17.

Avison, D. & Fitzgerald, G. (2003) *Information Systems Development: Methodologies, Techniques, and Tools*. McGraw-Hill, London.

Churchman, C.W. (1964) Managerial acceptance of scientific recommendations. *California Management Review*, 31–38.

Fortune, J. (1987) *Projects and Their Genesis*. Open University Press, Milton Keynes.

Fortune, J. & Peters, G. (1995) *Learning from Failure*. John Wiley & Sons, Chichester.

Imeson, M. (2003) Core systems – the risk angle. *The Banker*, 1 (Supplement), September.

Keil, M., Mann, J. & Rai, A. (2000) Why software projects escalate: An empirical analysis and test of four theoretical models. *MIS Quarterly*, 24: 631–664.

Larsen, M. & Myers, M. (1999) When success turns into failure: A package-driven process re-engineering project in the financial services industry. *Journal of Strategic Information Systems*, 8: 395–417.

Lyytinen, K. & Hirschheim, R. (1987) Information systems failures: A survey and classification of the empirical literature. In P. Zorkoczy (ed.) *Oxford Surveys in Information Technology*. Oxford University Press, Oxford, pp. 257–309.

MacLeod, D. (2004) E is for error. *The Guardian*, 8 June.

Mansell, G. (1993) The failures method and soft systems methodology. *Systemist*, 15: 190–204.

Mason, R. & Mitroff, I. (1981) *Challenging Strategic Planning Assumptions*. John Wiley & Sons, New York.

Mellahi, K. & Wilkinson, A. (2004) Organizational failure: A critique of recent research and a proposed integrative framework. *International Journal of Management Reviews*, 5–6: 21–41.

Naughton, J. & Peters, G. (1976) *Systems and Failures*. Open University Press, Milton Keynes.

Peters, G. (2003) Review of retooling: A historian confronts technological change. *Education Communication and Information*, 3 (2): 296–299.

Pinto, J.K. & Mantel, S.J. (1990) The causes of project failure. *IEEE Transactions on Engineering Management*, 37: 269–276.

Sauer, C. (1988) *The value of case studies in understanding organizational aspects of information systems*. Internal paper, Department of Computer Science, University of Western Australia.

Sauer, C. (1993) *Why Information Systems Fail: A Case Study Approach*. Alfred Waller, Henley on Thames.

Saunders, J. & Bloom, R. (2004) Five days of computer chaos leaves bank's clients in limbo. *The Globe and Mail, Toronto*, 4 June.

The Royal Academy of Engineering and The British Computer Society (2004) *The Challenges of Complex IT Projects*, www.raeng.org.uk, accessed 1 May 2004.

Vickers, G. (1981) Some implications of systems thinking. Reprinted in The Open Systems Group (eds) *Systems Behaviour*. Harper & Row, London, pp. 19–25.

Wateridge, J. (1997) How can IS/IT projects be measured for success? *International Journal of Project Management*, 16: 59–63.

Wedley, W.C. & Ferrie, A.E.J. (1978) Perceptual differences and effects on managerial participation on project implementation. *Journal of Operational Research*, 29: 199–204.

Williams, R. (2002) *Retooling: A Historian Confronts Technological Change*. MIT Press.

Chapter 3

CHALK AND CHEESE

Introduction

This chapter tells the stories of two projects, beginning with a brief outline of each before setting out more detailed chronologies and analyses. Unlike many reports of projects it is based entirely upon information that was gathered on site while the projects were actually being carried out.

These two particular projects were chosen for inclusion in a programme of research into 'real-life' project management because they were expected to be very similar. They were comparable in terms of size, scope and content and were based in the same type of organization. At the time access to them was being negotiated, they both looked equally likely to succeed; in the event, however, the outcomes of the two projects turned out to be very, very different. Project A was largely successful across the whole of the range of measures normally used to judge success. Project B exhibited most of the characteristics of failure: it was over budget, late and did not meet stakeholders' expectations. They thus started out as two pieces of chalk but they ended up as 'chalk and cheese'.

The projects

Project A

Project A began in the early autumn of 1998. It was carried out by a Government Agency within a large Department of State and its purpose was to set up the infrastructure in the form of a helpline to communicate information about a new piece of national legislation and enable the enforcement of the requirements of the legislation throughout the United Kingdom. The helpline and enforcement system had to be in place by April 1999 and the project as a whole was scheduled to come to an end two months later.

The success criteria laid down for the project were as follows:

- System to be fully operational by April 1999
- System to be produced to specified quality standards

- Project to be completed within budget
- System to fit in with the organization and other projects being undertaken by the organization
- All relevant staff to be adequately trained in the new system.

A team of 24 people from the senior levels of the Agency, its Department of State, and a second Department of State involved in the implementation of the legislation, was put together to act as the decision-makers for the project. This team will be referred to in this account as the Management Team. The Management Team members recognized that because they represented three different organizations, and were also dispersed geographically, they would need to establish robust line management reporting and decision-making processes. Their solution was to recognize two members as project champions and arrange the remaining members into a functional matrix.

An experienced Project Manager, appointed from within the organization, took up his responsibilities by the beginning of September 1998. He was placed in charge of the day-to-day management of the project and was supported by a core team of approximately 30 people, referred to here as the Project Team. The majority of the Project Team members were situated in the north of England on the same site as the Project Manager. Some members were based in the English midlands and the remainder were scattered around the UK.

The size of the budget remains confidential, but the Project Manager regarded the budget as generous when compared with the norm for comparable projects within the government department concerned.

An 'in-house' Project Management Method (similar to PRINCE), with which most of the core team members were familiar, was used to manage the project. Under its provisions a Project Board was in overall control of the undertaking, but day-to-day decisions were made by the Project Manager. He was responsible for ensuring that all people involved in the project knew what was expected of them. As prescribed by the method, the project was divided into the following stages:

- Initiation
- Research
- Investigation
- Feasibility

- Business Case
- Funding
- Design
- Development
- Implementation
- Closure.

During the course of the project it was felt that the method was 'too heavy' and required far too much documentation, so it was 'cut down'.

The software package 'Microsoft Project' was also used. Its main purpose was as a tracking tool to enable time taken and costing information to be tracked weekly. It was also used to identify dependencies and flag those regarded as 'critical'. The information it provided on project progress was fed back to the decision-makers.

Although there were some delays, unexpected events and setbacks during the course of the project, the project's owners, the Project Manager and the Project Team all regarded it as a success. It met the objectives that were set. By the appointed completion date of 1 April 1999, a telephone helpline, staffed by trained operatives able to offer information and advice, was operational and 14 teams of inspectors trained to carry out the necessary enforcement had been put in place in locations across the United Kingdom. The project was also within budget. The Closure stage was reached in May and a Post-Implementation Review was completed before the project was formally brought to a close as scheduled at the end of May, by which time the helpline and the inspection teams were already embedded in the organization and judged to be working well.

Project B

Project B was undertaken within a public sector organization employing around 220 people and run by a General Manager and three senior managers, who were known collectively as the Management Team. For the bulk of its work, the organization had contractual arrangements with four different Purchasers to provide services to Clients who were spread across a total of 80 Outlets. The organization's information system was central to its day-to-day operation but it also fulfilled a vital second role. Payments for the organization's services were triggered by the delivery of statistical reports to the Purchasers and these reports were based on data stored in the system.

The need for the project was identified initially as a result of concerns about 'Y2K' (year 2000) compliance. Doubts expressed internally about the ability of the current systems to withstand the 'millennium bug' had led to a firm of outside consultants being called in to carry out an information and communication review and recommend a strategy that would carry the organization forward into the next century.

The consultants concluded that a new information system was required. They recommended that this be based on the Internet as the 'key technology' and that it should have a new Windows-based database at its heart. The consultants also recommended that an experienced Project Manager who was a skilled IT professional should be appointed to oversee the work. They also pointed out that the Project Manager should have sufficient time available to devote to the role and possess adequate levels of authority to ensure that tasks allocated across the organization were managed effectively. The technical aspects of this proposal were adopted, but some of the advice on the qualities that the Project Manager should possess was not accepted. In July 1998 the job of managing the project was given to a member of staff who had the necessary IT skills but no project management experience. Four members of staff, only one of whom had professional IT qualifications, were assigned as assistants. This group will be referred to as the Project Team in this account. The Management Team, rather than the Project Manager, was to make the main decisions concerning the project and it was also decided that other staff would be co-opted onto the Project Team as and when necessary.

It was seen as essential to complete the project before the end of 1999 to avoid the potential 'Y2K' problems of the arrangements it was replacing. In order to meet this absolute deadline and fit in with other logistical considerations, a schedule was drawn up with a completion date of the end of August 1999. The life of the project was thus set at 14 months. The budget, which included the cost of supplying and installing a dedicated personal computer at each of 20 remote sites, but did not include any staff costs, was regarded as 'adequate'.

Use of the project management methodology PRINCE2 was considered, but in the end no formal methodology was used. 'Microsoft Project', of which none of the project team had any previous experience, was used to allow Gantt charts to be produced for scheduling purposes.

Although the start of the project had been scheduled for July 1998, the Project Manager and the members of his team were so busy with their routine duties that they could not hold their first Project Team meeting until the beginning of January 1999.

The main item on the agenda at the first meeting was the rescheduling of the project to meet the end of August deadline. It was not long before the project fell behind the revised schedule as a variety of problems began to emerge. The project was eventually completed at the end of February 2000. One of the primary aims, to put a new Windows-based database in place, was achieved eventually, but many other objectives were not met. Furthermore, the project exceeded its budget by around 25%. If staff costs had been included, the overshoot would have been even greater because a significant amount of overtime was worked as the schedule slipped further and further.

Unfortunately the completion of the project did not mean an end to the problems. A number of technical limitations/inadequacies to the new information system came to light soon after it began operation. The effect of these was to reduce the amount of activity the organization was able to undertake and this, in turn, led to a reduction in the organization's income. Many members of staff were unhappy with the new system. In part their dissatisfaction was due to their lack of training, but it was also triggered by their belief that their opinions had been ignored when design decisions were being made early in the project's life cycle.

Chronological history of Project A

The first three months (September–November 1998)

By the end of the first three months the project was progressing to plan. The Initiation, Research, Investigation and Feasibility stages had all been completed successfully and the Business Case stage was in progress. Throughout this period the Project Manager met with his Project Team at least once a week and also travelled to London to meet senior members of the Management Team on a weekly basis.

The next three months (December 1998–February 1999)

At the start of this period the Business Case stage was completed and approved. Set-up costs, covering the purchase of hardware and software and the payment of the Project Team's salaries, etc., were agreed with the Agency's Department of State. A 'Service Level Agreement', which specified running costs and performance targets to be met once the system was operational, was also drawn up.

During December, Parliament had been due to finalize certain rules and regulations connected to the legislation that was at the heart of this project. This timing fitted the projected timescale very well, but in the event some of the regulations promised for December were only agreed in the middle of February and others remained undecided for even longer. Some of the issues that were still outstanding posed no threat to the project's timing, but one or two of them did, and additional work on the part of the Project Team was needed to deal with the consequences of these delays. The biggest consequences were due to the follow-on effects that the delays had on plans to publicize the arrangements that were being made. For instance, in the absence of a planned advertising campaign that should have been triggered in December, it was necessary to organize a series of seminars and events across the country to draw attention to the forthcoming helpline.

Despite the delays at legislative level, the project's Design and Development stages were completed within this period. Originally it had been suggested that 16 members of staff would be needed to operate the system, but the Project Team decided to increase this number, first to 22 and then to 30, to be sure of being able to operate the helpline from 0800 to 2000 hours, seven days a week. As the helpline's first day of operation would be the day before a public holiday, it was decided to keep the helpline open over the holiday weekend. Contingency measures had then to be set in place to enable staff to be called in from a nearby call centre if the number of calls was higher than expected. To resolve a possible dispute with the newly appointed Helpline Unit Manager over the number of helpline staff to be trained, it was decided to train an additional 30 staff, bringing the total up to 60, thus providing cover for holidays and sickness. A 'language line' was also added to the system being developed.

By January 1999 orders for new equipment were in place and the Project Team had taken delivery of an 'off the shelf' software package consisting of a new database and management information system for tracking purposes. Work then commenced on customizing the software. An 'on-line script' was prepared for the helpline, and the internal recruitment of the staff who would operate the system was started. Training needs were identified and an organizational structure for managing the operators was also proposed.

Other government bodies became involved in the project and, as a result, some decisions about the operation of the system were revised. New risks and problems also emerged and had to be managed. One of these was the possibility that training would not be completed in time. The amount of time available for training was already tight, but failure to agree the final regulations delayed the start of training, making the time available even shorter. To help to overcome this problem it was decided to use outside contractors to put together the training manuals when the regulations were finally in place, thus getting the job done more quickly and freeing internal staff to begin their actual training. During the training period one of the trainers was 'pulled off' the project by another department. This problem was resolved by postponing the start of inspector training by one week.

The new enforcement system being put in place covered all parts of the UK. Just as the accommodation for the helpline staff was nearing completion during February, it was realized that there would be difficulties in providing accommodation for enforcement staff working in Northern Ireland's rural areas. Agreement was reached that they would work from home but, as a consequence, they would have to be provided with laptop computers and facilities for electronic communication.

The project's implementation stage was reached towards the end of February. The implementation plan allowed for 10 'Implementation Teams' (see Table 3.1), each led by a member of the Project Team who, in turn, reported to the Project Manager.

Table 3.1 Responsibilities of the implementation teams	
Team	Responsibilities
Technical	Regulations; Legislation; Amendments to legislation
Compliance	Instructions; Procedures, Field area; Appeals management
Business Side	Distribution of staff; Locations; Size of teams; Forms
Helpline	Procurement; Business instructions; Links with field; On-line guidance
Training	Helpline; Back office; Technician; Field
Human Resources	Recruitment; Job descriptions
Service Level Agreements	National management; Performance targets; Measurement targets; Business plans
Security	Data protection; Data integrity
Finance	Transfer of funds; Setting-up costs; Business case
Customer Service	Leaflets; Communication; Education; Events; Seminars

Spending was tracked weekly throughout the duration of the project. It was found during this period that although the cost of the project had risen considerably against the Project Manager's projection, it was still within the total budget allowed for it.

The final three months (March–May 1999)

The final legislation on which the project depended was approved by Parliament early in March and a document providing full guidance was made available by the middle of the month. This resolved all the uncertainties, so moves began to make up for lost time. The Department of State launched a television advertising campaign to publicize the forthcoming helpline and a copy of the training manual was made available on-line, pending the arrival of the printed versions, so that staff training could begin straight away.

By the middle of March arrangements had been made for the new software to be tested and put in place. The tests produced only 11 outstanding minor incident reports. To put this into perspective, when the Contributions Agency formally accepted their National Insurance Recording System 2 (NIRS2), there were 1589 outstanding incident reports (Collins, 1999).

By the end of March a 'health check' carried out by an independent auditor showed that the project was running on time and within budget and that the other targets specified in the business case were being met. At the beginning of April the helpline started answering calls as planned. The volume of calls received was largely as predicted until the first television advertisement was screened. The surge of calls that followed caused the system to 'crash' and calls were missed. The Project Team acted swiftly to prevent a recurrence. They obtained a list of times when the advertisement would be televised again and revised their operational plans accordingly. Although the number of calls continued to fluctuate widely, and rise dramatically after each television advertisement, no further calls were missed.

The closure stage of the project was reached during May and overall control of the operation passed from the Project Team. The team's final act before it was disbanded was to undertake a review of the management of the project. The lessons learned were recorded in 'Lessons Learned Files' and the Project Manager ensured that each member of the team had his or her 'Staff Training and Experience Record' updated to reflect the experience gained in undertaking the project. Finally, the Management

Team undertook a Post-Implementation Review and the project was closed formally at the end of May.

Chronological history of Project B

July–December 1998

Between the scheduled start date in July and the end of the year very little progress was made. At the end of June it was suddenly realized that many of the people with whom the organization would need to negotiate during the early stages of the project would not be available during the summer months, so the start would have to be delayed until the autumn. Come the autumn, however, the project still did not begin. October, November and December were the IT section's busiest months of the year as they were fully occupied extracting information from the current databases for the massive numbers of reports that had to be prepared on the previous year's activities. Furthermore, the Project Manager was still occupied full time in his role as Information Services Manager. The one positive move as far as the project was concerned was the decision, at the beginning of December, to advertise internally a temporary post (nine months) of Information and Marketing Manager to take over many of the Project Manager's existing responsibilities. The Project Manager would, however, still be required to oversee the IT side of the business as it was believed that he was the only person capable of doing this.

January–March 1999

At the beginning of January the Project Manager held his first meeting with the Project Team and rescheduled the project, compressing it down from 14 to eight months (January–August 1999). After the meeting he produced a Gantt chart listing the 123 tasks which he believed would have to be completed before the end of August if the project was to be finished on time. Data transfer from the old system to the new was scheduled for the first week in August. The chart was distributed to the Project Team during the second week in February.

Initial approaches to the Purchasers were made in January. It soon became clear that the Purchasers believed that only half of their Outlets would be in a position to provide a dedicated Internet line. As a result of this information the Management Team instructed the Project Manager to visit each of the 80 Outlets personally to ensure that they appreciated the benefits to be gained by providing Internet connectivity and would therefore take the steps needed to make a dedicated Internet line available. This was a very time-consuming exercise for the Project Manager, made more so because he did not drive and had therefore to use public transport.

By the end of February the Management Team had identified, for their new database, three potential suppliers, one of whom had supplied their existing database. Twelve staff members, representing the different sections of the organization, were invited to play a part in the evaluation and selection and attended demonstrations of the three different options. Meanwhile the Management Team had discovered that one of the three suppliers would only be willing to license the software for 30 people to access it simultaneously (the average number of people accessing the existing database simultaneously was 50) and that another could only provide very limited support facilities. This left just one supplier – the one that had supplied the existing database – on the Management Team's shortlist. Unfortunately this supplier's product was the one that was least preferred by the 12 staff members who had just attended the three demonstrations. Nevertheless, on the grounds that the project was already well behind schedule and that no further suppliers were being considered, the Management Team decided to award the contract to this supplier without further discussion. Indeed, the Management Team never offered an official explanation to the staff of the reasons for their choice of supplier.

By March it was obvious that the 'vision' of a dedicated Internet line in every Outlet's premises would not be realized but the good news was that the chosen supplier was in the process of developing software that would make it possible to replicate the database onto laptops for off-line use. It was therefore decided to use this option where no dedicated Internet lines were available, which made it necessary to purchase 50 laptops at an estimated additional cost of £70 000. As money had therefore to be saved elsewhere, the Management Team decided to opt for the data to be transferred between the old and new database through the process of 'data migration' rather than 'data translation'. Consequently certain codes attached to records on the old database would not then be searchable on the new database, but the Project Manager and his Team were not told of this decision until after the contract with the new supplier was signed.

By the end of March decisions had been made over equipment specification: equipment that could be refurbished had been identified, and orders placed for the necessary new equipment, such as a new database server which would be housed in the same location as the current database server, three miles away from the organization's headquarters. (This arrangement dated from the days when equipment such as servers had to be kept in air-conditioned premises.) During the last week in March the Project Manager held a second face-to-face meeting with his Project Team. (He normally communicated with team members by e-mail.) Following the meeting he produced a second Gantt chart, which suggested that the project was running approximately two weeks behind the compressed schedule and was therefore almost 30 weeks behind the original plan.

April–June 1999

The Project Manager continued his programme of visits to the Outlets. By the time he had finished he had found that only six of the 80 would be willing to provide dedicated Internet access and PCs, and a further six were offering to provide dial-up facilities that would be shared with other users. It thus became clear that the Consultants' plan of hosting a web server would not be economic. It was therefore decided to retain the present arrangement of offering 'static' Internet access through a website hosted by an outside company and to install further software (at a cost of £3000) on the new database server to enable the 12 Outlets with either dedicated Internet access or dial-up facilities to connect to the database through the Internet in 'real time'. Unfortunately, when the company currently hosting the organization's website was approached, it said it would not be in a position to extend the present contract. A search for a new Internet Service Provider (ISP) had to begin.

In April an evaluation copy of the new database was made available and the Project Team started to familiarize themselves with it. By the end of April delivery was taken of 80 new PCs and 50 laptops together with network cards, cabling and supporting software. The PCs and laptops all came with Windows pre-installed. The new machines were not compatible with the existing system without the installation of additional software, and to save time it was decided to store them until the new database came 'on line'. They were stored in the only secure area available, a room at the far end of a cellar that ran under the whole of the building into which they were to be installed.

In May, the Project Manager arranged for outside contractors to undertake the necessary rewiring of the building in preparation for the new system. This was completed by the third week in May. At the end of May the database supplier met the Project Team and demonstrated the capabilities and requirements of the new software. This enabled the Team to make decisions on the process of data migration and on the training required for the organization's staff. As a result of this meeting it became clear that the organization would not be in a position to have the new database in place by the end of August. It also became clear that coding problems resulting from the data migration process would not allow information for the statistical reports for 1999 to be extracted from the new database, so parallel running would be required until they had been completed.

The Project Manager called the third full Team meeting during the first week in June. Once again the project was rescheduled and a third Gantt chart was produced. The supplier was unable to carry out the data transfer process until the first week in September which would leave just one day for testing before the new system went live on 8 September. The new schedule was very tight. The Project Team of four people had just 11 weeks to undertake the following tasks:

- install a training database containing dummy records for staff training
- input codes, user information and mail-merge documents into the training database
- prepare a user manual, tutorials and case studies to be used in the training sessions
- train over 120 members of staff
- install the new database server
- set up the 80 new PCs and install software to allow them to be connected to the existing and the new databases
- remove all redundant/incorrect data from the existing database to ensure data integrity before the data transfer began.

July–September 1999

At the start of July the version of the database for training was installed. To save money it was only licensed for six concurrent users and hosted from a PC. It was decided that two trainers would be needed at each session and that the majority of staff would require two days training. This meant that it would be impossible to train everyone by the end of August even without delays. The training had to start immediately, even though the user manual, tutorials and case studies were not yet available. (A draft version of the user manual was distributed at the end of July.) Training was made even more difficult because the codes were not input into the training database until August.

It became clear to all that with the current arrangements it would be impossible for the training to be completed on time. A new training team, comprising six members of staff, was given two days training then made responsible for cascading the training to other staff.

During July, the Project Manager signed a contract with an ISP. The contract stipulated that the ISP would host the organization's website from 1 August 1999. By the first week in August the new database server, promised for the end of May, had still not arrived. When it did arrive during the third week in August it was found to be faulty.

Coincidentally, it had been decided to refurbish the organization's offices in August and make the first floor, where most of the system users were situated, 'open plan'. All the partitions were removed, together with much of the new wiring and junction boxes for the new system that had been installed in May. The resulting need for rewiring added to the expense of the project and delayed the installation of the furniture and PCs. Worse still, when the Project Team thought they would finally be able to install the new PCs they found that they could not be accessed as the whole of the cellar area in front of the door to the secure room where the PCs had been stored was now occupied by the old office furniture that had been removed from the first floor. It had been placed there by a removal firm on the instructions of one of the Management Team members, and the removal firm could not return to remove the furniture until the middle of September. Consequently, no new PCs were set up or installed until the final week in September. This delay, combined with the need to replace the faulty database server, forced the Project Manager to reschedule the date for data transfer yet again. The new date was the last week in October 1999.

October–December 1999

By the start of October a number of staff, including some key workers, had still not been trained. Two members of the Project Team were instructed to run a further six training sessions while the others set up user information for the new system and installed the new server. An attempt was made to remove redundant data from the old database in order to speed up the data transfer, but this task was never completed.

On 22 October data from the old database was sent to the supplier for transfer and the new database software program was installed on the server. Two members of staff were co-opted onto the Project Team and given the task of entering new codes and mail-merge documents into the new database. Owing to the vast amount of redundant data the data transfer process took a week and the data was downloaded onto the new server on Monday, 1 November 1999. No testing took place, and staff began to use the new system immediately. It soon became apparent that the codes and documents that had been set up during the previous week were not present. The Project Manager contacted the supplier who referred him to documentation dated 11 May 1999. This stated clearly that all codes and documents would be over-written during the data transfer process and that no one should be logged onto the system when the codes and documents were being inputted. The staff therefore had to stop using the new system until 15 November to enable all the set-up work to be done again. When they finally tried to log onto the system it was found that the majority of user passwords had been set up incorrectly, and rectification caused a further two days delay.

As the Project Manager did not have the necessary authority to issue orders to staff, he asked the Management Team to supply staff with clear instructions on how data should be recorded during the data transfer period. In particular, he requested that staff should be reminded that, for the present, both the old and the new systems had to be operated in parallel, and that staff must therefore ensure that they continued to enter certain categories of data into both systems until the end of the year. Unfortunately the instructions were only issued in the form of an e-mailed message, and the message itself was ambiguous. Many staff failed to read it and many of those who read it failed to understand it. In the absence of clear instructions they devised their own methods for dealing with the backlog of work that had accumulated. Some staff entered the most recent data first, and, on finding files missing, created new records. Other staff failed to check for previous data and added duplicate records as they worked through their backlogs.

At the end of November the Project Team ran the first data checks on the new system. They found that over 100 duplicate records had been created and that nearly three-quarters of the data would not be capable of being used correctly when the statistical reports were prepared because it had not been added to the system in chronological order.

By the second week in December it was clear that there were problems with the main Windows operating system. It was 'crashing' three or four times a day. Each time this occurred a member of the Project Team had to make the six-mile round trip to the server to reboot the system. The problem was eventually traced to the Wide Area Network's (WAN's) log-in procedure; people were not being logged out when they stopped using the system, so the limit set for the number allowed to use the system at the same time always appeared to be exceeded. Unfortunately, there was no support contract for the Windows system so the Management Team decided to send one of the Project Team on a course during January 2000 to learn how to configure the log-in process.

The final three months (January–March 2000)

On 31 December 1999 the licence for the old system expired but the important work on the statistical reports had not been done. As the year 2000 dawned it also became apparent that very few staff had continued the parallel entering of data into the old system. A team of staff was required to work overtime to enter the data and a two-month licence extension for the old system had to be negotiated.

During January 2000 a technical limitation to the database came to light. In order for staff to perform searches on records it was necessary to re-index the database every day. This process took two hours and while it was being carried out it slowed the system down substantially. An attempt was made to run the re-indexing during the night but this interfered with the backup procedures. Indexing therefore had to take place during the day, resulting in complaints from staff about the slowness of the system.

The start of February saw progress being made. The WAN's log-in system was repaired successfully and the old database was finally decommissioned. The six Outlets with dedicated Internet access were able to interact fully with the new database and the six with the non-dedicated lines were able to use the database whenever they could actually get on line. Unfortunately, the prospect of increasing the numbers beyond these in the near future looked very unlikely. The General Manager wrote to the remaining Outlets asking them to contact the organization when they were in a position to provide Internet access. In effect, he was reducing the scope of the project; connecting Outlets via the Internet was no longer falling within it.

Due to the many other problems that had been experienced, a number of security issues had been neglected. In February a request for funds to purchase an uninterruptible power supply and an 'updatable' brand of antivirus software to replace the current non-updatable version was rejected by the Management Team because the project was already over budget.

During the second week in February the laptop software arrived and was loaded onto two machines for testing. Severe problems soon emerged. A download of only 40 records took over three hours and caused frequent 'crashes' of the main system. The software supplier was consulted and it was discovered that the problem lay with the amount of free memory on the organization's database server. (Only half the amount of memory recommended by the suppliers had been purchased.) Further memory would need to be installed but financial constraints meant it could not be ordered until the start of the new financial year in just over a month's time. Despite the fact that the laptops were not operational, the Project Manager closed the project at the end of February.

No formal post-implementation review of the project was undertaken but many of the deficiencies associated with its outcomes were soon revealed because they led directly to a fall in the organization's income. Income was directly proportionate to the total amount of work done for the Outlets as recorded in the statistical reports. This amount fell for the following reasons:

1. Mistakes in the data due to essential fields not being completed. These resulted in work that had been done not being recorded.
2. Data 'lost' during the transfer period.
3. Staff spending less time working within the Outlets because they had to return to 'base' to input data.
4. System 'crashes' in the afternoons when most staff were trying to input data. These, too, led to work that had been done not being recorded.

Furthermore, two of the organization's contracts were not renewed at the beginning of January 2000 because the new system could no longer provide the information required. A third contract was only renewed after the organization agreed to set up a separate database to service it. At the same time as income fell, costs increased. The new system required considerably more maintenance than the previous system and maintenance had to take place out of business hours, thus requiring technicians to be paid extra to work in the evenings and at weekends.

Conclusion

As was stated at the beginning of this chapter, the similarities between Projects A and B were substantial when they were selected for study. Using the 'framework for examining success' given in Table 2.1, Table 3.2 looks at the extent to which the projects were successful. As can be seen, by the time both projects were finished the

Table 3.2 Application of project success criteria to Projects A and B

Project success criteria	Project A	Project B
Is completed	Yes	Yes, but scope reduced
Is well managed	Yes	No
Is within budget/schedule	Yes	No
Meets objectives (client requirements/organizational objectives)	Yes	No
Performs as intended/is technically sound/is appropriate	Yes	No
Does not display undesirable side-effects	Yes	No
Meets quality/safety standards	Yes	No
Fits in/adapts to its environment	Yes	No
Is used/supported	Yes	Used, but not supported
Provides intended/required business/other benefits	Yes	No
Fits in with the rest of the organization/causes minimal business disruption	Yes	No
Provides long-term benefits	Yes	No

differences between them could not have been greater. Across almost all criteria Project A was successful and Project B was not.

Reference

Collins, T. (1999) Problems with NIRS2 treble. *Computer Weekly*, 28 January, p. 3.

Chapter 4

SYSTEMS CONCEPTS

Introduction

The approach adopted in this book for the understanding of IS failures is based on a set of systems ideas and methods that have been developed and used in a wide range of settings. Indeed, they aim to be applicable as a framework for understanding any situation. This chapter lays the foundations and begins the process of building a toolchest of these systems ideas and techniques that can then be applied within an overall systems approach. The chapter discusses the key concepts that are fundamental to systems thinking and are necessary to gain full advantage from the approach. The chapter also considers the complexity that surrounds information systems which are central to this book. All the ideas introduced here have proved extremely useful, but occasionally some 'health warnings' are necessary.

Perception and appreciation

In Chapter 2, the ways in which failure and success are perceived emerged as an important theme in the consideration of information systems and, at the very end, the idea of an information system being embedded within a wider system, such as a work system, was introduced. The term 'work system', meaning a system within which human participants and/or machines perform a business process, represents a broader and more helpful viewpoint than the tight definition of an information system with which many readers will be familiar. Nevertheless, it still contains within it the idea that this business system exists in some objective sense. An alternative view, which is an essential aspect of the approach taken in this book, is that 'system' is a notion which is applied to a situation by an individual, often with the aim of understanding it or explaining it more easily. The difference in these two views – whether systems exist or not – is far more than a philosophical argument. It has practical implications for the way in which systems ideas are handled and it influences the extent to which the use of those ideas in a particular application can be regarded as valid.

For many who work closely with hardware and software systems the idea that a system is somehow ambiguous or exists solely in the eye of the beholder may seem strange. At first glance, it might seem like a step on the road to chaos. If a system does not exist, how can a team work together to produce something that is called a system, and how is it that all sorts of systems surround us and seem to work very well without anyone challenging their existence?

To take the view that a particular system exists implies two key assumptions. First, it implies that once the definition of a system has been agreed and the information about a candidate for the descriptor 'system' is known, there will be agreement about what it contains and all the interrelations within it; and, secondly, there is an assumption that a system has a concrete and unchanging form. So, inherent in the view that systems exist is not just the assumption that a concept such as system has a public currency, but also the view that individuals share a single unambiguous perception about the features of a specific situation. It is easier to see this distinction in the context of systems we meet every day rather than information systems. For example, the term 'system' is widely used in everyday speech in relation to transport or education, but while two people may complain about the poor state of the education system it is unlikely that they would both include the same features in their descriptions of this system. They may both recognize teachers and school premises as parts of the system but may disagree over the inclusion of parents, pupils, politicians, privately funded schools, publishers or broadcasters. Even when there is agreement over what constitutes the system, there is seldom a single view about the nature of the relationships between its components. It is much safer, therefore, to take the view that, although concepts such as component, subsystem and system itself may be defined, they will be applied by individuals to different features of a specific context. Thus, whatever one's views on the philosophical argument about whether systems are or are not constructs, it is, as a matter of practical expediency, better to subscribe to the view that the systems identified for the purpose of analysis do not actually exist as systems. Instead it is safer to assume that certain individuals are deciding to treat particular features of a situation as if they conform to a (sometimes personal) set of rules and definitions for the concept 'system'.

Now for a health warning: when these ideas are applied, they are often found to be particularly rewarding and capable of providing powerful insights. In such circumstances, it is remarkably tempting for the practitioner to slide into a way of working that comes close to assuming that the systems do actually have some objective reality. The authors of this book are firmly of the opinion that systems are only constructs – indeed, one of the strengths of the idea is that what is taken to constitute the system can be experimented with and changed. However, there will sometimes be a close and deceptive correspondence between the elements that the practitioner would choose to group together and consider as a system, and the items that might commonly be called a system. Experience suggests that it is all too easy to describe and write about systems as though they exist, and the linguistic manoeuvres required to avoid this misrepresentation can become very tedious. Therefore, the words used to identify, describe or investigate systems in this book may not always remind the reader of the authors' standpoint despite our best intentions. Furthermore, when other authors are quoted it will not always be known or made explicit how they are using such terms, so particular caution will sometimes be needed.

The term 'system' refers to an 'organized whole' or a set of components that are interconnected. The decision as to which, if any, aspects of a scenario can be regarded as constituting a system will depend upon the interest and background of the viewer as well as the purpose of the study. Vickers (1984) developed a sophisticated notion of 'appreciative system' to describe a state of readiness to distinguish some aspects of a situation rather than others, and to classify and value these in this way rather than that, and he began to explore how one acquired an appreciative system and how it changes with experience. In applying systems ideas it is important that analysts are not only aware of their own appreciative systems that give rise to the values and norms they apply, but are also aware of the appreciative systems of other participants in the situation.

A simpler but related concept is *weltanschauung*, the German word for 'world view', which in general usage refers to a personal philosophy of life and the universe. It is used in much the same way by systems practitioners to make explicit their view that different individuals have a distinct set of values, different perceptions and distinct expectations. An appreciative system and *weltanschauung* thus both attempt to provide mechanisms which explain why perceptions and interpretations differ from individual to individual.

The concepts of *weltanschauung* and appreciative system provide far greater insight than simply helping us to understand why different stakeholders may judge the same set of events or processes and reach different conclusions about their performance. The concepts also help to explain why apparent agreement about objectives for a project may disguise differing assumptions about the context, the wider goals, the resources needed and even the status of any agreement.

Holism

The two fundamental aspects of a systems approach are organization and wholeness; consideration of the whole is an essential precursor to considering individual parts. A systems perspective thus has to start from trying to ensure that all the likely angles have been covered, all the potentially fruitful ways of looking at a situation have been explored, and all the features that may be relevant have been examined. Note that in this last sentence the word 'all' has been deliberately qualified by 'likely', 'potentially fruitful' and 'may be relevant'. It is neither feasible nor desirable to examine every feature of a situation whatever its relevance. It is always necessary to employ judgement, but one important aspect of a systems approach is this striving for a comprehensive overview of relevant aspects before any detailed investigation is undertaken. This deliberate taking of an overview is commonly called *holism*.

Readers should note that there is also a more specialized use of the term 'holism'. Checkland (1981) would wish to reserve use of the term 'holism' for the far more precise scientific sense of being concerned with wholes, as opposed to a reductionist approach which builds up understanding and models from the individual parts. This is not the usage adopted here where the term 'system' is used to mean discrete but interconnected entities.

Now for another health warning: the concepts presented in this chapter have been refined by different authors. They are interrelated: on certain issues they overlap, and on others they can complement each other. This can be a strength; for example, there is an interesting practical link between *weltanschauung* and *holism*. One approach to building a more holistic understanding is to look at a situation from a variety of standpoints. Churchman (1971) and others explicitly use these multiple and contrasting *weltanschauungen* to widen their conception of a problem and build a broad holistic insight.

Environment and boundary

If a system is to be identified and considered as a clearly defined entity within some context, then it needs to be distinguished from its surroundings. This requires two further concepts: environment and boundary. The boundary is the imaginary line which delineates what is considered to be the system from that which is outside.

However, the environment is not the rest of the world; whether something is judged to be part of the environment is determined by whether or not it influences or is influenced by the system that has been perceived. The environment can also exert a degree of control over the system, but while the environment can be influenced by the system it cannot be controlled by the system.

These three basic concepts of system, boundary and environment are remarkably powerful tools for reaching an understanding of or explaining failures in information and other systems. Project A in Chapter 3 provided an example of an information system development that went remarkably well, but it was introduced to work alongside some legislative changes. The project plan had to take cognizance of uncertainties both in the timetable and in the content of the final legislation. Parliament was not under the control of the project team but its actions needed to be included in their thinking and planning. Parliament and its processes, ministers, civil servants, etc., can be seen to have been considered as a part of the environment in this case. In plenty of other situations, however, changes in legislation and the regulatory environment that occur after a project commences or an IS is implemented may not have been considered as a part of the environment, and an IS initiative or the business it supports may become unusable or require wholesale reworking. In Project B it seems unlikely that the public transport infrastructure of the region was considered as an important aspect of the environment, and yet it proved to be so – particularly once it was decided that each of the 80 sites should be visited by a key member of the team who did not drive.

Hierarchy

Chapter 2 introduced the idea of the embedded nature of systems. That idea is included in the concepts of system and environment, but it is also embraced by the concept of hierarchy. The systems that we consider at any particular time will be both built up of subsystems, which could themselves be considered as systems for certain purposes, and be a part of some wider system. These systems are nested together and are interconnected somewhat in the way that a software system has a suite of programs within it. However, the hierarchical nature of systems within systems and the iterative way in which they interconnect is an important feature and leads to systems producing behaviours that are more or less than the sum total of their individual components. As Vickers (1981, p. 21) states:

It is less, because organization constrains. Elements in a system are not free to do all the things which, unorganized, they might do. It is more because, when organized they are enabled to do together what none of them could do alone, or if unorganized, even together.

In the case of an IS development project, hierarchy can readily be seen in the monitoring and control arrangements. A project will be monitored by the project team informally and formally and both individually and collectively. The team will report on progress, perhaps to a project board, which will also look at other measures of activity, such as project expenditure. In turn, different parts of the organization will be watching activities in their different ways. At each level in the hierarchy, there will also be differing types of action available in the light of the feedback.

Open systems, closed systems and groupthink

The concept of environment brings with it the theoretical possibility that a system might not have an environment. Such theoretical abstractions have proved useful in physics and thermodynamics. A system that does not interact with anything else, and therefore does not have an environment, is termed a 'closed system'. It is difficult to imagine a scenario in which – while trying to be holistic – it proved to be insightful or useful to consider a system as closed. However, if a system could be considered as closed, it would have very different properties from the more normal open system. Because a theoretically closed system imports or exports nothing – not even energy, materials or ideas from its surroundings – the second law of thermodynamics says that it can only deteriorate. This disorder is called *entropy*, and in a closed system it can only increase. In other words, things can only deteriorate, at least to the point where any order is simply the result of random activity.

In practice, systems containing humans are bound to be open in the technical sense, but the concepts of open and closed provide useful analogies. So, an analyst will want to consider an IS development in its context, but it may be helpful to consider whether the actors in a situation considered the system to be closed or open. Did they, for example, feel able to import resources, ideas or energy if needed? Project B in the previous chapter seemed to have little freedom to import resources or expertise, to such an extent that at the end it was not possible to buy antivirus software.

One extreme example of the way in which the concept has provided a penetrating explanation of human behaviour is the work of Kirschman-Anderson (1980). She was seeking to understand the Jonestown massacre in which 913 followers of the Reverend Jim Jones' religious cult 'The People's Temple' died, apparently after drinking a mixture of cyanide and soft drink. She found that systems concepts like open and closed systems and entropy provided an adequate framework for analysis and explanation. Her use of the closed system mirrors the groupthink symptom of closed-mindedness described below. Put simply, a group exhibits groupthink when it considers the outside world and environment less and less, tends to overestimate its own power and morality, and then becomes inclined to ignore the ethical or moral consequences of its decisions.

All IS activity involves people working together, often in teams. Social psychologists have long considered the way in which people interact in small groups a fascinating topic of inquiry. A small group can be defined as a dynamic system of interaction between at least two people. Group life involves a continuous process of adaptation by individuals to one another and to their mutual needs and problems (Lewin, 1948). Social psychology has been much concerned with this level of human activity in a variety of contexts, stretching from therapy groups to factory production teams. One important aspect of this work has been the development of models of successful groups. Since a successful group is defined as one that succeeds at its tasks, then it is not surprising that a group that is deemed to be successful has members who place a high value on their membership of the team. A successful group can, therefore, be judged, at least to a partial extent, according to the level of allegiance that individuals within it feel to one another. In many aspects of human existence, being a part of a successful group can be regarded as crucial. Drug-takers or alcoholics, for example, may be helped to modify their behaviour by becoming members of a group which they value highly and which frowns upon the behaviour they have previously exhibited. Similarly, a small company may be more successful in business terms if everyone within it feels part of a team and works closely with other members to achieve the best for each other and the group. Research into both successful and problematic IS developments often point to teamwork and interaction between groups as an important feature.

In general, those groups that are found to be most successful display certain characteristics. For example, a successful group is likely to feel autonomous from its surroundings, with an obvious boundary surrounding the group which makes clear who is inside the group and who is outside. It is also found that the more difficult it is to obtain entry to a group, the more membership of it is valued.

Strong groups also display behaviour that encourages members of the group to conform to the group's own view of the world. Members develop a stereotypical view of outsiders, and put internal pressure on members who do not share the group view of a situation. Although the origin of this and similar findings is work with successful groups, an observed and important downside of their success is that strong group coherence – and other attributes associated with it – can result in the group becoming less successful at dealing with environmental changes and the task in hand. Janis (1972, 1982) has, in the context of work on public policy-making, given the name 'groupthink' to this phenomenon. He uses it to refer to 'a mode of thinking that people engage in when they are deeply involved in a cohesive in-group, when members' strivings for unanimity override their motivation to realistically appraise alternative courses of action'. He goes on to say that groupthink 'refers to a deterioration of mental efficiency, reality testing, and moral judgement that results from in-group pressures' (Janis, 1972, p. 9).

Janis has examined a series of American policy 'fiascos', and discovered strong evidence for groupthink with defective decisions being seen to arise from very cohesive groups. The examples he cites include the Kennedy administration's unsuccessful orchestration of the Bay of Pigs invasion of Cuba and the attack on the US Navy at Pearl Harbor by the Japanese. Unfortunately, even if groupthink provided a perfect explanation of poor decision-making it would be difficult to establish that it was occurring because, as Janis acknowledges, the link between decision-making and outcomes is itself not perfect. A sound decision may still result in a *débâcle* if poorly implemented, and a flawed decision may still be followed by a successful outcome if luck or the behaviour of others has a major, beneficial impact. However, by looking at fiascos and policy successes, Janis has been able to arrive at eight symptoms that help to define the groupthink syndrome, and has combined them to form three main types, as summarized in Table 4.1.

Although Janis developed this framework in the context of US policy-making, it has not proved at all difficult for him to extend the model to the UK. He considered the members of the Chamberlain Government's inner circle who supported the policy of appeasement and concluded that they were probably dominated by groupthink. Fortune and Peters (1995) have posited that groupthink provided a partial explanation of the introduction of the Poll Tax (Community Charge) and the events leading to the subsequent downfall of the then Prime Minister, Margaret Thatcher.

'Is he one of us?' was asked by Mrs Thatcher of colleagues about other colleagues... The criteria were political or economic rather than social. 'Wet'

Table 4.1 Symptoms of groupthink (after Janis, 1982)

Type I: Overestimates of the group: its power and morality
1. An illusion of invulnerability, which creates excessive optimism and encourages taking extreme risks.
2. An unquestioned belief in the group's inherent morality, inclining the members to ignore the ethical or moral consequences of their decisions.

Type II: Closed-mindedness
3. Collective efforts to rationalize an order to discount warnings or other information that might lead the members to reconsider their assumptions before they recommit themselves to their past policy decisions.
4. Stereotyped views of enemy leaders as too evil, weak or stupid to counter the risky attempts to defeat their purposes.

Type III: Pressures toward uniformity
5. Self-censorship of deviation from apparent group consensus, thereby minimizing the importance of any self doubt.
6. Shared illusion of unanimity partially resulting from self-censorship and partially from the false assumption that silence means consent.
7. Direct pressure for loyalty on members expressing arguments counter to the prevailing view.
8. The emergence of 'mindguards' who protect the group from adverse information.

---

was used by her to rebuke colleagues who lacked her singleness of purpose or disagreed with her economic or social policy.

(Watkins, 1991)

Luckily, IS projects and business systems do not normally exhibit the extreme behaviour found in the Jonestown massacre or the Office of the Prime Minister. However, several of the large-scale corporate failures of the early part of this millennium seemed to include an assumption, by tightly knit groups of executives, that they were able to operate outside the normal rules that governed others.

In the IS context, it is all too easy for a team – whether it is the software developers, one of the project teams, or a whole company – to only look inwards and consider that it should only attend to the things it can control. In practice, sticking entirely to the role, however tightly it is defined, is a risky strategy.

Systemic and systematic

Like many other systems methods, the Systems Failures Approach is both systemic and systematic. Both these features have system at their core, but there the similarity ends. *Systemic* means pertaining to a system. In this case it means an approach that applies the concept 'system' – and related systems ideas such as those mentioned already – to an actual or potential IS failure. *Systematic* means organized and following a pattern. All but the most chaotic or creative of methods would be systematic, incorporating procedures that are to be adhered to, even if they also allow multiple branching and a variety of paths running through them. One of the advantages of a systematic approach is that it causes users to follow a path that may force them to confront difficult but important issues. A further advantage is that it allows someone else to examine the way in which the method has been applied, and by examining the process arrive at some view of the likelihood that the application was sufficiently comprehensive to warrant confidence. These features would be true of most methods; it is the systemic aspects of a systems approach that make it distinctive. The approach described in Chapters 6 and 7 is systemic in the classic sense. Put simply, it involves expressing a situation in systems language and then, once a system has been identified, scrutinizing it, first to see if it holds up as a system and, secondly, to see how it compares with an idealized model of a system.

Further concepts

Individual concepts can be exceptionally powerful. Whole nations can be transformed by ideas such as freedom, equality or human rights, and individuals' behaviour can be altered radically by notions such as evil or justice. Similarly, systems concepts can provide a powerful set of tools for thought and, when carefully applied, can generate considerable insight. Experience suggests that even the few that have already been included in this chapter, such as system, holism, boundary, environment, open and closed, will unlock many scenarios.

Table 4.2 A system of systems concepts (after Ackoff, 1971)	
Concept group	**Concepts**
Systems	Abstract system; Concrete system; System state; System environment; State of System; Closed system; Open system; System event; Static (one-state) system; Dynamic (multi-state); Homeostatic system
System changes	Reaction; Response; Act; Behaviour
Behavioural classification of systems	State-maintaining system; Goal-seeking system; Process; Multi-goal-seeking; Purposive system; Purposeful system Relative value of outcome; Goal; Objective; Ideal; Ideal-seeking
System relationship concepts	Variety
Adaptation and learning	Function; Efficiency; Learn
Organizations	Control(s); Organization

However, there are many other systems concepts that can at times prove useful. Ackoff (1971) identifies a group of 32 concepts and terms which he organizes into 'a system of systems concepts' and groups under headings such as system changes, behavioural classification of systems, and adaptation and learning (see Table 4.2).

In effect this is an alternative way of organizing an earlier set of concepts mapped by Young (1964) (see Figure 4.1).

By no means are all of these concepts applicable in an IS or in a business setting. For example, during the study of a failure in a part of an organization, the initial conceptualization of a system might suggest that there is an explanatory advantage in considering the type of system it is deemed to be. There might be a *prima facie* case for deciding whether it could be considered to be a state maintaining system, and thus so fixed in its ways that it could only return to its previous state, or a multi-goal-seeking system which thus had the freedom to yield different outcomes in response to changes in its environment. Distinctions such as these might appear to provide a useful way of exploring system behaviour in some circumstances. However, in the authors' experience little additional interpretation or explanation is gained beyond the

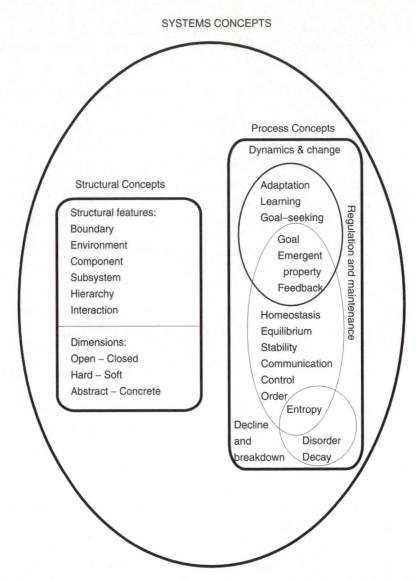

Figure 4.1 A map of the main systems concepts using the categories of Young (1964) (after Cameron, 1983)

acquisition of a label. Furthermore, Ackoff's definitions of these particular concepts, which at first glance look relevant, cannot be applied to any systems that have the ability to learn and adapt. So, Ackoff's multi-goal-seeking systems are in fact ones that are restricted to a particular type of response to changes in their environment; they can vary the actions they take, but the outcomes of those different actions are predetermined by the environmental change. Of all the many systems classified by Ackoff, it is only those that are labelled 'purposeful' that include people who play a part in determining behaviour and outcome.

Communications, knowledge and 'sensemaking'

Whenever an inquiry is set up into something that has gone wrong, whether it is a computer system or a police investigation, there always appears to have been a breakdown in communications. Research into IS failures is no different. Curtis, Krasner, and Iscoe (1988), for example, researched a set of large-scale software projects and analysed them according to five levels: the individual, the team, the project, the company and the business milieu. They identified three recurring problems in designing these systems: the thin spread of application domain knowledge; fluctuating and conflicting requirements; and communications bottlenecks and breakdowns.

Even at a most simple level, it is easy to see why communications in large-scale projects can be problematic. A small team of four people would only need six one-to-one meetings for everyone to have met with everyone else, but a team of eight people would require 28 such meetings and a team of 16 would require 120. Curtis, Krasner and Iscoe (1988) quote one team member thus,

> In the beginning ... there were 3 of us. How many lines of communications are there, 1, 2, 3? But once you go up to 15 people it can get out of hand ... In the beginning it was easy to keep track of what was going on. It was only after reaching the critical mass ... that things began falling into the cracks, and we were losing track ... There was just too much going on.

Large-scale IS projects therefore need both informal and formal communications processes if they are to stand any chance of being successful, and communications are closely linked to the ideas of open and closed systems. When a system has been conceived it will then have both a structure and a set of processes that flow through that structure. Since this entire book is about information systems, it will be self-evident that information and information flows are important. It is information that is communicated, and that information is not just data; it has meaning, and it is the meaning that is crucial in both the design of information systems and their development.

Rather than use the term 'information', it is helpful to think of knowledge and intelligence in the military sense of carefully weighed and considered information as being a key aspect of IS development. This idea links well with all three of the findings of Curtis, Krasner and Iscoe. For example, they see the thin spread of knowledge about the different areas (domains) of knowledge needed for a large-scale development to be an issue. However, they also observed the mirror image: that exceptional designers were skilled at communicating their technical vision. Furthermore, they quote Weinberg (1971), who suggests that those who are perceived as most knowledgeable become communications focal points and, hence, more knowledgeable and more able to integrate. So knowledge and communications go hand-in-hand in both successful IS as well as other projects. The third finding of Curtis, Krasner and Iscoe, about fluctuating and conflicting requirements, considered how the need to stabilize requirements – in order to design and build – is at odds with the desire to be responsive to changing market and other conditions. They observe again that the communications and coordination processes became crucial to coping with the incessant fluctuation and conflict among requirements.

How people deal with ambiguity, for example over requirements, is what Weick (1995) has called 'sensemaking'. It operates at an individual level and can also be applied in an organizational setting. At the individual level, there are seven key aspects to sensemaking, which are detailed in Table 4.3.

There is a clear link between what Weick calls sensemaking and what Vickers sees as an individual's appreciative system. Both are about taking personal experience and that of others and using it not only to interpret a current situation but also to modify how one looks at things in the future.

Weick uses the ideas of sensemaking in organizational contexts as well as those of individuals, and he has identified a number of ways in which organizations tacitly codify past knowledge and experience (see Table 4.4).

Control

When things go wrong we often refer to them as being 'out of control'. By this we can mean either that this inability to influence events is itself a failing or that this loss of control could lead to other things going awry. It is usually, but not always, possible to distinguish between the two! As well as this colloquial meaning, the term 'control' has an historical engineering meaning. For centuries, engineers have incorporated control devices into the design of machines, and their various control models have proved to have explanatory power in other domains such as management and biology.

Table 4.3 Sensemaking in an individual context (after Craig-Lees, 2001)

1. *It is grounded in construction of an individual's own identity*   The sensemaker has as a key task the establishment and maintenance of his/her own identity. Sensemakers are seen as being part of an ongoing puzzle as they continually redefine their identity and decide which of several possible 'selfs' is appropriate to present to others. A person's changing sense of self is posited to operate in the service of three self-derived needs: need for self enhancement; the self-efficacy motive; and the need for self consistency.
2. *Retrospective*   Since people only know what they are doing after they have done it, the creation of meaning involves attention to what has already occurred, even if only seconds before. Secondly, whatever is seen to be occurring will be influenced by what has gone before. Furthermore, what people react to is already a memory.
3. *Enactive of sensible environments*   Since, people influence their own environment, they shape and are shaped by the context in which all sensemaking occurs.
4. *Social*   Sensemaking is a social process because an individual is part of networks which have shared meanings, and are sustained through the development and use of common language.
5. *Ongoing*   Sensemaking is a dynamic process which neither starts nor stops, so people extract cues from continuous flows of activity.
6. *Focused on and by extracted cues*   Sensemaking tends to be swift, and so what can be observed is the product rather than the process.
7. *Driven by plausibility rather than accuracy*   Because people are exposed to multiple cues, with multiple potential meanings, they need to filter and select and interpret, and so the precise accuracy of an observation is secondary to its plausibility and acceptability.

In systems terms, control is an action that a system or subsystem applies to its own activities in order to reach or maintain a desired state. For the purposes considered here, the need for control is brought about either by the influence of the environment on the activities that are being undertaken or by variations within a subsystem which are due to its complexity or to its stochastic nature. Control is achieved either by modifying activities or by changing inputs.

Table 4.4   Sensemaking in an organizational context (after Weick, 1995)

- *Ideology*   Shared, relatively coherent, emotionally charged beliefs, values, norms, cause–effect relationships, preferences for certain outcomes, and expectations that bind the organization together. They provide ready-made interpretation structures for supporting the belief side of sensemaking.
- *Third-order controls*   Unspoken organizational premises (jargon, patterns of uncertainty absorption, unique communication channels, informal procedures, and personnel selection criteria) that shape the flow/content of information, constrain the search for options, focus the definition of risk, and constrain expectations. They act to delimit the belief side of sensemaking.
- *Paradigms*   Internally consistent sets of simplifying heuristics about important objects in the world, how these objects act, how they relate to one another, and how they come to be known. They serve as alternative realities for linking belief and action.
- *Theories of Action*   Organization-level cognitive structures that filter and interpret environmental signals as triggers for organizational response. They link perception to shaping action.
- *Tradition*   Symbolic mental structures (patterns of action, patterns of means–ends behaviour, organizational structures) that facilitate an action-oriented stance towards the world. They provide the ready-made formulas for action.
- *Stories*   Narrative structures that represent filtered, ordered, and affected accounts of experience based on a 'beginning–middle–end' story sequence. They are used to guide action under conditions of crisis, complexity and time pressure.

Classical feedback control, also often known as the engineering control model, is depicted in Figure 4.2. Essentially, this model assumes that the aim is to reduce and ideally eliminate any discrepancies between what is actually observed as the output of a system or subsystem and the target. (This is sometimes referred to as error-nulling.) The outputs, such as the time taken to process a set of data, are measured continuously or periodically and these measurements are compared with the desired values, or reference levels. As a result, the activities of the subsystem or the inputs to it can be modified (increased, reduced, or their nature changed) in order to bring the outputs to their desired levels.

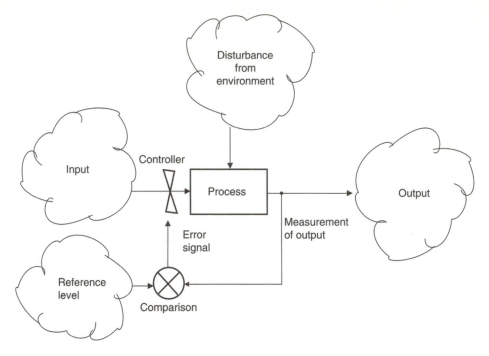

Figure 4.2   Classical feedback control

Good-quality feedback may seem to be an entirely helpful attribute, but it does not necessarily result in corrective action; indeed, one major cause of failure can be instability due to what is termed 'positive feedback'. In feedback control, the information that is fed back results in corrective action. This type of feedback is termed 'negative feedback', but in positive feedback the signal that is fed back leads to actions that increase the deviation from the desired level. As Dhillon and Ward (2002) point out, the instability resulting from positive feedback makes forecasting impossible. For example, a petrol retailing system would normally operate with a large number of individual decision-takers acting independently. However, if there were rumours of a blockade of refineries in protest at prices, motorists who normally drove with petrol tanks less than half-full would flock in great numbers to fill their tanks, thus guaranteeing that the rumoured shortage would occur. This example is illustrated in Figure 4.3.

Even in well-designed control systems, and especially in large and complex transformation processes, there is often a delay between the output being measured and the control actions taking effect. Therefore it is necessary to take account of the dynamics

Figure 4.3   Positive feedback loop for petrol shortage

of the activities being controlled in order to prevent too-frequent control actions or over-compensation that will then lead to new deviations from the desired level.

Poor communication within a feedback loop can also lead to a variety of problems. 'Open loop' or 'broken loop' control results when no information about the current state of the output is received by the decision-taker and no informed control actions are possible. If information collected about the current state becomes distorted, 'control' actions may be taken that cause the outputs to deviate even further from the desired state. If information relayed about the outputs of a process is accompanied by amplified 'noise', inappropriate control actions may be triggered which may in turn cause severe random variations in the output. Such variations may be greater than those caused by the influence of disturbances from the environment.

These difficulties can be seen in computerized commercial information systems where data that is inputted or processed incorrectly gives rise to misleading answers when databases are interrogated. As research has shown (see, for example, Koester & Luthans, 1979), the authority carried by computer-generated information – just because it is computer-generated – renders it less liable to challenge.

In practice, in information systems and other complex human endeavours it is not possible to directly measure the outputs. As Yolles (1999, p. 143) states, it is necessary 'to determine measures that are representative indications of the output' and specify the reference levels in terms of 'social and cultural norms, behavioural norms or standards'

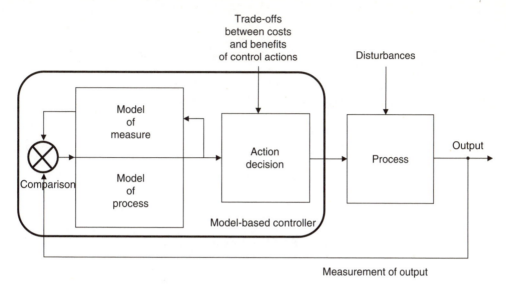

Figure 4.4 Modern feedback control

that may be perceived differently by different observers. These performance measures and performance indicators may take time to collect and analyse, and any action may not be fully effective immediately. Therefore, in so-called modern feedback control (see Figure 4.4), action is based not on simple error-nulling but on the best estimate of the true current state and the likely effects of any changes. The best estimate is generated within the control system itself, using a model of the system. This internal model, which is continually updated to reflect the changes that are taking place, evaluates the various control actions that could be taken to examine the trade-off between each action's effectiveness and associated costs.

In both types of feedback control, the emphasis is on reacting to events after they have happened. In certain situations, however, disturbances can be anticipated and steps taken to counter them before they affect output. Setting up action in the absence of any feedback is called *feedforward* control, as shown in Figure 4.5. In certain circumstances it, too, can be effective. For example, one may anticipate a mismatch between income and expenditure after retirement and begin to save now in order to be able to supplement income to match expenditure later. Feedforward control is sometimes used in combination with feedback.

For control to be completely and successfully established and consistently maintained, a number of preconditions would need to be satisfied:

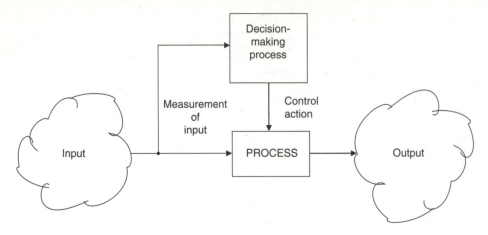

Figure 4.5 Feedforward control

1. The processes being controlled must be understood, at least to some degree. The inputs that affect the outputs, and the directions in which they cause variation, must be known.
2. An appropriate form of control must have been selected.
3. It must be possible to sample the inputs and outputs repeatedly and at suitable intervals.
4. There must be adequate communication between the measuring mechanisms and the decision-taker.
5. The reference levels must be achievable and must be specified in forms that are compatible with those in which the outputs are to be measured.
6. The changes in the level of inputs must not be greater than the range of variation for which control actions are capable of counteracting disturbances.
7. The time interval between a measurement being taken and control action being initiated must be appropriate.
8. The decision-taker must be of an appropriate level of sophistication for the activities and/or processes being controlled.
9. Agreement must be reached over what constitutes an acceptable trade-off between error, resources required and timing.

In passing it is worth noting that the notion of controllability and the preconditions of successful control could be applied to the process through which an organization or society learns from its mistakes and failures. For example, items 3, 4 and 7 in the above list, when taken together, imply that analysis of failures, and hence knowledge about them, must be timely and open and available to those responsible for decision-making. Indeed, for more complex systems, Volta (1988) has proposed an extension of the cybernetic-based models of control. He suggests that control be regarded as 'triggering actions that modify behaviour' and that 'control is activation, by internal factors, of the evolution of a system in a given direction' with communication being 'one of the basic mechanisms of activation'. He links this with the concept of controllability and states that 'a system is controllable not only when it allows recovery, after an error, but when it is capable of being improved through errors'. Thus, in Volta's terms, a complex system that lacks controllability is not learning and is susceptible to failure.

A final health warning: control models were, of course, originally derived from engineering perspectives in which the purpose of a control device is to ensure that the system or subsystem moves towards the goals that have been set for it, i.e. they are purposive. In an organizational context, however, there can be a more sophisticated form of control in which a purposeful system, such as an organization, selects different goals in the light of knowledge about environmental conditions and the way they are changing.

Conclusion

The concepts in this chapter are applicable to the process of understanding failures in IS and in their development. For example, the design of an IS may have taken insufficient account of the environment in which it is to operate, or the team managing the work on the project may have not set up appropriate mechanisms for collecting feedback about progress.

References

Ackoff, R.L. (1971) Towards a system of systems concepts. *Management Science*, 17: 661–671.

Cameron, S. (1983) *Systems Approaches*. Open University Press, Milton Keynes.

Checkland, P.B. (1981) *Systems Thinking, Systems Practice*. John Wiley & Sons, Chichester.

Churchman, C.W. (1971) *The Design of Inquiring Systems*. Basic Books, New York.

Craig-Lees, M. (2001) Sense making: Trojan horse? Pandora's box? *Psychology and Marketing*, 18: 513–526.

Curtis, B., Krasner, H. & Iscoe, N. (1988) A field study of the software design process for large systems. *Communications of the ACM*, 31: 1268–1287.

Dhillon, G. & Ward, J. (2002) Chaos theory as a framework for studying information systems. *Information Resources Management Journal*, 15: 5–13.

Fortune, J. & Peters, G. (1995) *Learning from Failure*. John Wiley & Sons, Chichester.

Janis, I. (1972) *Victims of Groupthink*. Houghton Mifflin, Boston.

Janis, I. (1982) *Groupthink: Psychological Studies of Policy Decisions and Fiascoes*. Houghton Mifflin, Boston.

Kirschman-Anderson, E. (1980) Jamestown, Guyana – a systems autopsy. *24th Annual Meeting of the Society for General Systems Research, SGSR*. Louisville, USA.

Koester, R. & Luthans, F. (1979) The impact of the computer on the choice activity of decision makers. *Academy of Management Journal*, 22: 416–422.

Lewin, K. (1948) *Resolving Social Conflict*. Harper, New York.

Vickers, G. (1984) Ecology, planning, and the American dream (1963). Reprinted in The Open Systems Group (eds) *The Vickers Papers*. Harper & Row, London.

Vickers, G. (1981) Some implications of systems thinking. Reprinted in The Open Systems Group (eds) *Systems Behaviour*. Harper & Row, London, pp. 19–25.

Volta, G. (1988) *Safety control and new paradigms in systems science*. Position Paper for World Bank Workshop on Safety Control and Risk Management, Washington, 18–20 October.

Watkins, A. (1991) *A Conservative Coup: The Fall of Margaret Thatcher*. Duckworth, London.

Weick, K.E. (1995) *Sensemaking in Organizations*. Sage, Thousand Oaks, CA.

Weinberg, G. (1971) *The Psychology of Computer Programming*. Van Nostrand Reinhold Co., New York.

Yolles, M. (1999) *Management Systems*. Pitman, London.

Young, O.R. (1964) General systems. *Yearbook of the Society for General Systems Research*, 9: 61.

Chapter 5

CAPSA

Introduction

The University of Cambridge is an 800-year-old institution with a world-class reputation for teaching and research. For example, in a 2001 survey looking at the quality of research in UK universities it was ranked number one overall and no fewer than 30 individual departments were given the highest possible rating. (For comparison, the London School of Economics and Political Science came second overall, with seven individual departments being given the highest rating; and the University of Oxford came third, with 25 individual departments being given the highest rating.) It is therefore perhaps not surprising that two reports published in the University's own official journal, *Cambridge University Reporter*, on 2 November 2001 provoked a storm of bad publicity in that day's national press. Coverage was widespread:

A Cambridge course in wasting £10 million – *Daily Mail*

Cambridge fails computer test – *The Guardian*

Cambridge finances 'a disaster bordering on farce' – *The Independent*

Cambridge University computer system 'a disaster' – *Financial Times*

First class blunders cost Cambridge £10 million – *Daily Telegraph*

The subject of the reports was the University's new on-line commitment accounting software system. The name given to the project to develop and implement the system was CAPSA. (CAPSA sounds like an acronym, but it isn't; the system took its name from a Roman book storage box.) The first report (Finkelstein, 2001) looked at the project and the operational system, CUFS (Cambridge University Finance System), that resulted from it. The second report (Shattock, 2001) examined the project in relation to its wider University management setting. This chapter is based on both those reports. CUFS was supposed to improve financial management within the University by allowing it to run its accounts in a way that makes it possible to see how much of each budget has actually been spent and how much of it has been committed. Instead it ended up with a system that was unreliable and difficult to use and, in practice, not actually delivering commitment accounting. This chapter thus tells the story of an information system project that failed across a wide range of criteria. First, it cost significantly more than had initially been envisaged. (Over £9 million had been spent by 2001 compared with an estimate of £4 million in 1996.) Secondly, it failed to meet the requirements set for it. A report to the University published in May 2002 found that CAPSA's performance did not measure up to its promise in a number of ways. One key failure it highlights is as follows.

> Nor has the system made 'commitment accounting' a reality. Commitment accounting means running accounts in a way that makes it possible to see how much of a fund has been committed, as well as how much of it has actually been spent. This is possible only to the extent that the system is used to place orders as well as to pay bills. Because placing orders through the system is as time-consuming and complicated as paying bills, it is widespread (and wholly understandable) practice in the University to bypass CUFS when placing orders.
>
> (Report of the Board of Scrutiny on CAPSA, 2002, para. 4)

Thirdly, the implementation of the system led to significant disruption to the working of the University to the point where the integrity of its accounting was compromised. For example, staff were unable to access research budgets and by 2002 there were still significant problems with the research grants module:

> It is the 'research grants module', the part of the system that supposedly handles research grants, that is still particularly unsatisfactory, and potentially undermines the integrity of the University's financial and management information systems. Its data structure is different from, and incompatible with, the data structure of the other modules, and, to make matters worse, the software is faulty.
>
> (Report of the Board of Scrutiny on CAPSA, 2002, para. 5)

Governance of the University

In organizational terms, the University of Cambridge is large and complex with over 160 departments and 30 Colleges. All of its teaching was once carried out by the Colleges, but now the University has expanded its role through the provision of facilities such as teaching and research labs to the point where Colleges are supplementing teaching rather than being the sole providers. However, it remains the case that every student has to belong to a College and Colleges are responsible for selecting, admitting and accommodating all undergraduates. The administrative load of the institution is thus shared between the Colleges and the University. Despite this additional complexity, Cambridge spends relatively little on administration. Shattock provides data (para. 2.1) to demonstrate this point:

> The percentage of reported total University expenditure devoted to the staffing costs of administration and central services was 2.6% in 1994–5, 2.6% in 1995–6, 2.7% in 1996–7, 2.7% in 1997–8, 3.0% in 1998–9 and 2.9% in 1999–2000 as against an average for English universities over the same period of 5.8%.

He also makes (para. 2.3) a comparison with Warwick University, of which he was Registrar. In 2001 Warwick had a turnover of a little under half that of Cambridge, but at the same time had twice as many qualified accountants working in its central finance office.

The University of Cambridge's principal executive and policy-making body is the Council. This is made up of the Chancellor (an honorary position), the Vice-Chancellor (who occupies the Chair) and 19 members elected every four years to represent various groups. The Registrary is the Secretary to the Council and head of University administration. The Finance Committee is one of the Council's most important standing committees. It too is chaired by the Vice-Chancellor and has the Treasurer as its secretary. The other central body is the General Board of Faculties. It is responsible for the teaching and research programme and advises the University on educational policy.

The University's ultimate governing body, equivalent to its parliament, is the Regent House. (The Vice-Chancellor is responsible to the Regent House, rather than to the Council.) It is a 3200 strong body of senior academics and administrators and most of its business is conducted at a distance through the use of Graces and Reports. A Grace is a proposal, usually from the Council, that a certain decision be made. Each Grace is published in *Cambridge University Reporter* and is deemed to be accepted if not challenged within 10 days by at least 10 members of the Regent House. Graces that are challenged are either resubmitted in modified form or put to postal ballot. Matters that are too complicated to be dealt with by Graces become the subject of Reports. These are published in *Cambridge University Reporter* and then debated publicly in the University's Senate House. A response is generated to the debate and published as a Notice, again in the *Reporter*, together with a resubmission of the proposal in the original Report, or perhaps in modified form, for approval without dissent or by ballot if sufficient members of the Regent House request it.

One of the ways in which the Council's accountability to the Regent House is enforced is through the submission of an annual report for examination by the Board of Scrutiny. The Board consists of eight elected members of the Regent House, two Proctors and two Pro-Proctors. (The Proctors and Pro-Proctors are officials elected annually by the Regent House.) Another body with an overseeing role is the Audit Committee. This is another standing committee of the Council. The rules in place at the time the reports on CAPSA were presented stated that it had to consist of eight persons appointed by the Council, of whom at least three had to be members of the Council, with provision for not more than two further persons to be co-opted and that at least two members of the Audit Committee had to have experience of finance, accounting, or auditing. The reviews by Finkelstein and Shattock were jointly commissioned by the Audit Committee and the Board of Scrutiny, so their reports were addressed to these bodies when they were published in the *Reporter*.

Before CAPSA

The University's first computer-based accounting system, which used flat file storage for data, was introduced in 1966. With some minimal evolution in functionality it remained operational for over a decade and a half, finally being decommissioned in June 1993. It was replaced by a system built on top of a relational database management system, referred to in Finkelstein's report by the name 'Legacy'.

Throughout its life, Legacy was subject to continuous evolution. One of the most significant enhancements that was proposed was the introduction of commitment accounting, and in late 1995 a working group, CAWG (Commitment Accounting Working Group), was set up to investigate. CAWG was chaired by a management accountant who had recently been appointed as an Assistant Treasurer. By late 1996 CAWG had developed proposals for the introduction of commitment accounting in the form of a lightweight front-end system based on Microsoft Access that would be developed in-house and designed to synchronize with Legacy.

A consultancy firm that specialized in advising charitable organizations, and had expertise in supporting medium-sized Microsoft-based accounting solutions, was called in to look at CAWG's proposal and provide an independent view of the broad functional requirements and feasibility of a 'standardized' commitment accounting system. After a three-day evaluation had been conducted, a report supporting CAWG's proposal was presented in December 1996. The proposal was costed at £377 000, including £110 000 for hardware in Departments.

In January 1997 a formal proposal went before the University's Resources Committee and the Joint Committee on Central Administrative Computing. According to Shattock (para. 2.7) the minutes of the meeting show that it was proposed that a 'front end' should link the system with the University's existing Oracle-based accounts system and that a cost–benefit analysis of the proposal suggested that savings of £1.5 million per annum could eventually be achieved. The proposal was approved and the allocation of the £377 000 needed to provide the system was granted. Shattock also points out (para. 3.2) that at this time, and for the next two years, responsibility for the project appeared to lie with the Treasurer, with the project being run on a day-to-day basis by the management accountant who had been appointed as an Assistant Treasurer even though the Deputy Treasurer was responsible for the management of the University's finances.

By the middle of 1997 two additional analyst programmers had been recruited to the University's Administrative Computing Unit to work with some existing members of the Legacy team on the development of the new system. Before long the project gained the name CAPSA and the consultancy firm that had conducted the evaluation was given the job of providing the commitment modules of the system.

Rethinking the project

In late 1997 a meeting of the people who would be using the new system was held. This was followed by a second meeting to obtain the views of Departmental Computing Officers. Their views were not positive. They expressed many technical criticisms of the new system, most of which centred on important non-functional requirements such as performance, security, connectivity and platform constraints. In the light of these, an internal Administrative Computing Unit review was conducted, but unfortunately this also raised doubts about the system, pointing, in particular, to the lack of involvement of the prospective users. It was decided to seek an external review.

The person chosen to conduct the external review was a director of a small business systems and project management consultancy. A large part of the work she did involved investigating users' requirements and working practices. A survey was carried out and meetings were held with staff in academic units. As Finkelstein points out (para. 8.6) the review did not include a systematic or complete business process analysis, but it did, according to Shattock (para. 2.10), release 'a surge of departmental demands, many of which were inconsistent and not compatible with the installation of a new integrated system'.

The consultant presented her interim report at the end of May 1998. It was not good news for the Chair of CAWG or the Treasurer. As it suggested that the new system being developed would not be able to meet expectations, work on the system was suspended. A CAPSA Management Committee was formed, consisting of representatives of the Administrative Computing Unit and other members of the Finance Division. This was nominally chaired by the Deputy Treasurer but, in practice, it was chaired by the Chair of CAWG who, together with the consultant who had conducted the external review, began to look for alternative solutions. They made preliminary analyses of the products on offer by a variety of major suppliers and talked to other higher educational institutions who had introduced or were in the process of introducing similar systems.

In July 1998 a report was issued to the Joint Committee on Administrative Computing. It rehearsed the shortcomings of the current situation and concluded that the developments that had been underway would neither meet the requirements of audit nor provide sufficient financial transparency. It recommended that instead of proceeding with its current plans the University should acquire an integrated, off-the-shelf 'industry-standard' accounting package. In line with this suggestion, the Finance Committee was asked to provide funds to support the development of a 'functional and technical specification'.

The bid was successful. A circular from the Treasurer dated 22 July 1998 announced:

> The Departments' needs proved to be so extensive that the review inevitably changed its focus to bring into consideration the replacement of the entire accounting system rather than adding a Commitment Accounting module to the existing structure.... It is evident that this approach is fully backed by

Departments who see it as being the only way forward to achieve responsible accounting to their users.

(Finance Division Circular C25(98), quoted in Shattock, para. 2.8)

Starting again

The CAPSA project restarted. The first step was to find a suitable software package. Requirements working groups, including a technical working group of Departmental Computing Officers, were set up. An implementation plan was also developed. This assumed a phased implementation of new functionality with the system being rolled out gradually across the University.

The potential suppliers considered in the preliminary analysis in June were gradually whittled down to two: SAP and Oracle (both US companies). SAP and Oracle visited the University to demonstrate their products using examples of typical workflows and user interfaces. They also provided large-scale public presentations which were attended by a wide range of University staff. Members of key working groups visited reference sites recommended by SAP and Oracle, but Finkelstein reports (para. 7.28):

> None of the visits was successful. In the case of SAP because no truly comparable reference appeared to be available. A 48-hour visit to see Oracle Financials at California Institute of Technology (CalTech) was arranged. As the system was not actually fully operational little was learned from the visit. Members of the working party were, however, struck by the vast effort devoted to the business process mapping activity being undertaken by CalTech staff and by warnings about the research grants module. Unfortunately these critical observations got lost in the jet-lagged confusion of the visit.

Departments were selected to test generic versions of the core functions of each potential supplier's products. The Department of Engineering (representing a large user) and The Fitzwilliam Museum (representing a small user) were chosen to test Oracle Financials, while the Department of Pathology and the Programme for Industry Office were to test SAP's recommended solution. This testing did not occur in the manner intended. Oracle did give access to a remote system, and staff in the two Departments chosen to test its product saw detailed demonstrations, but SAP was only able to offer further demonstrations of industrial implementations. Despite this the reactions of the departmental users of both systems were sufficiently positive to enable both potential suppliers to move into the next selection stage. Oracle and SAP were asked to review the University's requirements and provide an undertaking that they could support them. Both reported a 'line-by-line' match between the implicit and the explicit requirements and the processes supported by their systems and, as a result, both were asked to quote for supplying a system to meet the requirements. A hardware selection exercise was also carried out, leading to the recommendation of a Sun platform and the infrastructure requirements, particularly the service provider requirements, were considered.

Oracle provided a quotation that was substantially lower than that of SAP, and during October 1998 another report was submitted to the Joint Committee on Central Administrative Computing. This set out:

- the requirements
- a functional specification based on those requirements
- a standard weighted checklist assessment of the competing solutions
- the recommendation that Oracle be nominated preferred supplier.

The recommendation that Oracle be nominated preferred supplier was accepted by the Committee and the target date to begin rolling out the system was set for 1 August 2000. However, the Committee also recommended a further three- to six-month investigation to refine the specification in certain areas and that senior members of the University's management team should be closely involved in determining and monitoring the management issues arising out of the project.

The Committee's views went forward to the Finance Committee, where they were formally approved. However, Shattock also points out (para. 3.6) that:

> The relevant minute makes it clear that no contract should be signed with Oracle until the Committee, and the Planning and Resources Committee, on behalf of the Council, were satisfied by a final report. No report came back to the Finance Committee, however, but in the meantime the Planning and Resources Committee, at its meetings on 9 December 1998 and 15 February 1999, went ahead to allocate the funding, accept a cost–benefit analysis which was later shown to be fallacious, and approve the appointment of a project manager.

At this point in the proceedings SAP, the other potential supplier, raised objections to the procurement process on the grounds that it breached EU regulations on procurement. Fearing a legal challenge, the University reopened the process. Repeat tenders were considered under a framework agreement managed by a Third Party procurement agency but, once again, Oracle was chosen as the preferred supplier.

The funding allocated to the project was £4.3 million until it was realized that the amount of value added tax (VAT) had not been calculated correctly and the figure had to be increased to £4.72 million. Because of the way the project had grown, this large sum was unplanned expenditure. Therefore, when the Planning and Resources Committee agreed to this sum they also stipulated that it should be taken from the equivalent of the University's current account and a sinking fund established to pay it back over the next 10 years. (It is worth noting here that no such fund was ever established. Furthermore, the additional cost of the project, i.e. the £4.72 million allocated, was paid out of the University's reserves.) The University was, of course, expecting significant financial benefits from the introduction of the system. Based on a cost–benefit review (paper PRC(84)) presented to the University on 15 February 1999, the Planning and Resources Committee concluded that: 'The project should pay for itself by the end of the third year, by which time over £5 million of savings should have been achieved' (minutes of a meeting of the Planning and Resources Committee, 15 February 1999, quoted in Shattock, para. 2.14).

The aims and benefits of the project were set out in the following terms:

> The CAPSA Project will implement an integrated University Accounting Man-
> agement Information System that will assist the University of Cambridge to
> maintain the quality of its teaching and research into the new millennium.
> UFS will deliver to you consistent, up-to-date information that will be easily
> accessible from a system, which will be simple to operate for all authorized
> members of staff. It will incorporate on-line policy, procedures, and instruc-
> tions for users to follow. The University staff have been fully involved in every
> stage of the design of the system, and the selection of contractors. The system
> will be designed to be flexible and powerful enough to meet the expressed
> needs of every Faculty and Department in the University. The benefits UFS
> will bring include:
>
> - Commitment accounting – actual expenditure plus the value of unfilled
>   orders (sales and purchases).

- Greater control over research grants and departmental expenditure.
- A much greater range of information readily available.
- Clearer (customized) presentation of data allowing much improved monitoring.
- Integration of all forms of data – financial, stock, student registrations, etc., allowing powerful analysis, management reporting, what-if calculations, and more.
- Minimization of paperwork.
- Minimization of multiple entering of data.
- Internal transfers fully electronic.
- Data on supplier prices visible to all staff, thus reducing costs to even the smallest departments.

(Reproduced in Report of the Board of Scrutiny on CAPSA, 2002, para. 2)

Not everyone was equally sanguine. Shattock (para. 5.15) draws attention to issues of concern that had been raised at a meeting of the Audit Committee in December 1998. These include:

- realism over the timescale of the implementation
- the need to conduct a full and appropriate assessment of risks
- the need to clarify the cost benefits
- identification of post-implementation costs
- the need to manage change within the University (both in terms of business systems and cultural change)
- ability to secure appropriate and high-calibre staff for the project team
- capacity for departments to release the number of staff required; and the broad structure of the project team.

Shattock (para. 5.15) also states that:

In the discussion the [Audit] Committee noted 'that Enterprise Resource Projects (ERPs) were notorious for their late delivery' and were concerned at the 'extremely short timescale envisaged'. They also 'questioned the assumption made that all departments would be keen and willing to take on board a new, centralised accounting system'.

The most serious of the Audit Committee's concerns had been drawn to the attention of the Vice-Chancellor, the Treasurer and the Registrary in a letter addressed to the Registrary on 21 December. A certain amount of correspondence had ensued, the upshot of which was an admission from the Registrary that he could not 'provide full reassurance on the points you raise'. However, the Audit Committee had allowed the matter to drop and had not drawn attention to it in its Annual Report for 1998–9. By the end of February 1999 contractual exchange between Oracle and the University was underway.

Perhaps the reason why the Audit Committee wrote to the Registrary rather than elsewhere is that organizational changes that had started in 1998 had shifted responsibility for the project. A Management Information Services Division (MISD) had been set up to replace the Administrative Computing Unit and provide a more strategic view of the University's management information needs. Its formation swept away the Joint Committee on Administrative Computing and the direct line connection between CAPSA and the Treasurer because MISD reported to the Registrary.

The Director of MISD was a new appointee, recruited from the property services industry, who took up his post at the beginning of January 1999. Clearly, this was at a time when important discussions about CAPSA were taking place but there appears to have been a lack of clarity about the role he was expected to fulfil in relation to the project. Finkelstein (para 7.35) explains:

> It was expected by the Principal Officers of the University [the Vice-Chancellor, the Treasurer and the Registrary] that the active management of the CAPSA project from the University standpoint would be undertaken by him [the Director of MISD]. In retrospect it is less clear whether the new appointee understood this to be the case or, if he did, fully grasped the consequences.

Shattock (para 3.5) supplies further detail:

> The Director of MISD told me emphatically in the very brief conversation I had with him that he was only responsible for 'pay and rations' for the project and that his Deputy was actually in charge. .... It was reported to me by several people that [he] was not even aware of the CAPSA project until after he had taken up his post.

At the same meeting at which the Planning and Resources Committee had allocated funding to the project in December 1998, it had also agreed that an External Project

Manager should be appointed. The director of the small business systems and project management consultancy who had conducted the external review in May 1998 was selected. Her contract specified that she had full responsibility for delivering the project on time and within budget and that she should report to the Director of MISD.

A CAPSA Steering Committee was set up and held its first meeting on 22 March 1999. It comprised a senior academic as Chairman, the Director of MISD, the External Project Manager, the Treasurer, representatives of the acting internal auditors, a senior representative of Oracle, and various Faculty representatives, all of whom had a particular interest in accounting issues. According to Shattock (para. 3.3), its terms of reference were as follows:

1. To receive monthly reports from the [External] Project Manager on the progress of the implementation and to compare this with the implementation plan.
2. To consider and approve any necessary departure from the plan especially in the light of implications for the final target date.
3. To approve single items of expenditure in excess of £50 000 or to agree delegation of this responsibility to the Director of MISD.
4. To provide quarterly reports to the Principal Officers for onward transmission to the Central Bodies.
5. To draft a final Report on the implementation of the CAPSA system for publication.

Two methodologies were to be used alongside each other to manage the project. These were Oracle's own Application Implementation Methodology (AIM) and PRINCE2 (PRojects IN Controlled Environments version 2). AIM is a proven approach for implementing packaged applications. It divides a project into six phases:

1. *Definition* – gather information about the old system and the functional objectives of the new system.
2. *Operations analysis* – contrast the business needs with the basic Oracle application to determine the matches and discrepancies.
3. *Solution design* – prepare functional and technical specifications for the new system.
4. *Build* – implement the design specifications by converting data and coding interfaces and begin testing.
5. *Transition* – deploy the new system and run it in parallel with the old while continuing testing and conversion of the final data from the old system into the new.

6. *Production* – change from the old system to the new system and carry out any refinements and performance enhancements.

PRINCE2 was devised by CCTA, the UK government centre for information systems. It emphasizes the following:

- Organization through the setting up of a management structure comprising a Project Executive, a Project Board, a Project Manager, a Project Assurance Team and a Project Team.
- Planning, which covers the activities of estimating, collating, sequencing, scheduling and assigning resources.
- Controls of quality, progress and exceptions, all with their own reporting procedures.

Finkelstein (para. 8.13), however, raises doubts over the degree of rigour with which the methodologies were used:

> Though the implementation was ostensibly to be controlled using a well recognized project management method, PRINCE2, there is little evidence that this was properly established, or used with the rigour that such methods demand. The implementation method, AIM, is powerful and provides the skilled implementor with a large number of valuable resources. The method is, however, driven by document templates which need to be used with considerable care. I am not confident that in the early stages of the project AIM was properly used. During the entire project and throughout every phase, though large amounts of detailed documentation were produced, there is little by way of high-level overview. Both project and technical managers appear to have had difficulty in abstracting away from the immediate technical minutiae of the project to establish the big picture necessary for sound decision-making and control.

The CAPSA project team consisted of five people from MISD and between eight and 12 people seconded from other University Departments on a full- or part-time basis. Most of the team were not qualified accountants. Indeed there were only four qualified accountants in the central Finance Division team that was involved in CAPSA. Three of the four were granted early retirement at the end of July 1999 and the fourth resigned around the same time. Consultants supplemented the internal employees on the project team. In the early stages people from the External Project

Manager's consultancy firm provided secretarial and other services. Oracle provided an implementation team consisting of Oracle project management and technical staff, some of whom had technical expertise in particular Oracle Financials modules. As the project progressed, further technical consultants, most of whom were independent contractors, were brought in to cover technical shortfalls. Finkelstein points to tensions between these groups and conflicts and low morale caused by 'a failure to resolve issues of managerial responsibility and control' (para. 7.45).

The team was housed in a new building some distance from both MISD and the Finance Division. At the time the team was formed there were no computers, network connections or telephone lines in its new office space and it took almost five months to put everything in place.

A new problem

Despite the difficulties, progress was made on a number of technical issues, including system interfaces, arrangements for parallel running and stock coding, but this began to be overshadowed by growing awareness of a significant problem. The CAPSA implementation plan had been based on the assumption that a fundamental aspect of the accounting system, the Chart of Accounts (the account coding scheme on which a general ledger is based) would be unchanged in the new system, but this assumption was proving to be invalid. This was a severe setback. The response was to set up an Accounting Policy subcommittee of the CAPSA Steering Committee to formulate accounting policy and steer the project in relation to accounting matters, including the creation of a new Chart of Accounts. This subcommittee began work in June 1999.

At the end of that month a new Finance Director took up her post and almost immediately began investigations to determine the current status of the CAPSA project. This review confirmed the need for a new Chart of Accounts and revealed that due to this and other factors the cost of the project was rising from £4.72 million to over £8 million. At around the same time, the Director of MISD, who was also worried about lack of progress and rising costs, had instigated a short review of the project control systems by the University's external auditors. Their report was highly critical, not only in relation to project control issues, but also to the lack of University involvement in project planning, and of many of the project's assumptions, describing some of them as naïve. The conclusion of the report was that 'in its current form, the project is unlikely to succeed' (Shattock, para. 2.16).

The External Project Manager resigned. On her departure a joint report prepared by the Director of MISD and the Finance Director summarizing the current state of the project drew attention to many failings. Record-keeping, communications, management style, use and management of contract consultants, clarity of deliverables, financial monitoring and decisions about accounting policy were all criticized. A month later (that is, September 1999) the erstwhile chair of CAWG also departed, in his case to take up a post at another University.

Following the departure of the External Project Manager, a senior member of MISD who had been involved in the hardware and infrastructure aspects of the project took over as Project Manager, but not for long. The Director of MISD and the Finance Director, supported by the Treasurer and the Registrary, decided to appoint the Oracle practice of the University's external auditors to manage the project. The Steering Committee was advised of the appointment on 6 September and invited to authorize it, which it did on 18 October, but by then the new management team had been in place for over a month.

The new management team was headed by a Project Manager, a Technical Manager and a Change Manager. Theoretically the Project Manager still reported to the Director of MISD and the CAPSA Steering Committee but, in reality, many of the decisions were reached jointly at regular meetings of the Project Manager, the Director of MISD and the Finance Director. In addition, the Accounting Policy subcommittee of the CAPSA Steering Committee, which had the Finance Director as one of its leading players, began to act as the major customer of the project.

Within the wider project team there were also significant changes. The external technical consultants were dismissed to cut costs and the remaining members were reorganized. Effective management and control mechanisms were also established. However, Finkelstein (para. 8.17) levels significant criticisms at the new regime:

> On taking over, they [the new management team] failed to pick up the threads of the project and to use the work that had already been performed. They failed to manage the documented requirements or to assess the consequences of making changes to those requirements, a breach of the discipline of requirements traceability. They failed to identify or manage relationships with many of the key project stakeholders. They paid only lip service to risk management.

The new management team took over less than a year before the new information system was due to start rolling out, and two factors had combined to make the agreed timetable unachievable: first, progress was slower than anticipated; and, secondly, the need for a new Chart of Accounts meant that the overall size of the project had increased substantially.

The Project Manager, the Director of MISD, the Finance Director and the Accounting Policy subcommittee all agreed to abandon the plans for a phased roll-out and adopt a 'big-bang' approach instead. However, the 1 August 2000 deadline remained in force. It was also decided to reduce the scope of the system by removing not only the large number of external system interfaces that had been planned, but also the web user interface and lightweight access for occasional users which many Departments had said they wanted. A proposal was also made, for accounting purposes, to group smaller units within the University together under the umbrella of School offices, but this was rejected.

Work continued at a rapid pace within the project team and in the Finance Division, but other parts of the University were beginning to suspect that the project was in trouble and a series of CAPSA roadshows held in the last full week of January 2000 seemed to confirm these suspicions:

> The roadshow, intended to demonstrate CAPSA functionality and capture interest, seems to have had precisely the reverse effect. To a large audience of junior staff and many of the influential Departmental Computing Officers, who would be required to ensure that the 'client-side' of CAPSA operated, a static set of screendumps was presented, few questions were answered. Most attendees left with a strong sense of disquiet, many commented on the absence of the senior University staff who might have been able to lend credibility to the project.
>
> (Finkelstein, para. 7.63)

As the project progressed further, work on configuring the system started throwing up substantial numbers of bugs, both minor and major, to the point where identifying them, tracking them from the project side and applying patches began to take up almost all the time of the Oracle consultants. Worse still, as the CAPSA team became more and more overstretched, work in resolving the bugs became less effective with patches being dropped or misapplied.

The project's technical problems were compounded by staffing difficulties. During this period these were reported to the CAPSA Steering Committee on 10 January, 14 February, 14 March, 17 April and 15 May, when the Finance Director reported she had 19 vacancies in her Division, all of which needed to be filled by 1 August.

The schedule slipped further still. The window available for the testing phase became narrower and narrower. Effective integration testing became very difficult because there was no stable set of baselines across the project. Volume testing could not be carried out because of the fluidity of the system, and rigorous regression testing was completely impossible.

Early in May 2000 a demonstration showing the operation of the system in a typical Department was set up for the Departmental Computing Officers. This revealed two major problems. First, it showed that there were important shortcomings in the CAPSA strategy for handling heterogeneous client platforms. Secondly, the reductions in scope that had been decided a few months earlier were revealed to the Departmental Computing Officers for the first time, and they were the very people who had requested those functions in the first place.

With alarm bells ringing, project meetings were held in April with a view to identifying a fall back position in the event that CAPSA could not go-live in August. But in the end the only outcome of these deliberations was the decision to rely on Oracle's ability to fix the bugs in time.

By late May 2000 reports from within the project team were signalling a high risk that user requirements would not be met and that by August there would still be sufficient bugs in the system to impede critical functions. At the end of June 2000 a report to the Audit Committee from the internal auditors highlighted the dilemma facing the project. Shattock (para. 2.20) quotes from it thus:

> The project team has formed the view that if Oracle make insufficient progress in fixing the problems identified within a set timetable, a decision may need to [be] taken to defer the project and not go live on 1 August. There are serious implications attached to this: There is a reluctance to run with two financial systems in any one financial year. If 1 August 2000 is not achieved, there is a suggestion that the next possible implementation date is 1 August 2001. There would be a loss of momentum and enthusiasm for CAPSA as a result which could mean:

additional cost;

a need to retrain and retest;

having to support the existing systems for another year;

knock-on impacts on other projects.

We are not aware that detailed contingency plans have been developed to manage possible delays in the project, either for the full one year being suggested or for any interim period.

By the end of June the project team was more optimistic that the bugs were being corrected and it began to undertake some user acceptance testing. However, time was very short and due to problems such as finding sufficient representative data to populate the system the user acceptance testing was never completed. None of the users in the areas selected for the trials signed-off the system. Nonetheless, the next stage began: user training. Oracle training consultants were brought in to do this but unfortunately it was not without problems of its own. These included:

- Content insufficiently related to the work of the University.
- Many of the example transactions used were too simplistic and/or unrepresentative.
- Very wide variation in level of computer literacy between trainees in the same group.
- Technical hitches such as crashing and locking up during training sessions.

By early July few arrangements had been put in place to support users after the system had gone live. Temporary clerical staff had to be recruited to provide first-level support, such as answering immediate technical questions, in order to leave the CAPSA implementation team free to concentrate on more technically demanding issues that required longer term resolution.

Going live

At the end of July 2000 the weekly project meeting decided that the acceptance criteria had been met and approval was given for the system to go live. On 1 August Legacy ceased operation and CAPSA took its place. The Oracle technical consultants who had been working on implementation left and the longer term Oracle support scheme was put into place. A few weeks later the project was handed over to the University. In the absence, due to ill-health, of the Director of MISD, the Finance Director took charge. But all was not well.

Immediately after go-live, the system slowed to a crawl and so many people asked for help that the first-level support team was only able to provide call-logging. The CAPSA implementation team was also overwhelmed by cries for help. For the first six weeks of 'operation' the system was virtually unusable and users grew increasingly irate. One of the main problems was that the system had not been configured for the correct number of concurrent users but no sooner had it been reconfigured to remedy this problem than a bug arose as a consequence of the interaction between subledger security arrangements and caching.

Over time, staff from Oracle and a subcontracted database administration service were able to resolve the performance problems. However, the need to fix bugs continued well into the autumn and the CAPSA team did not have sufficient people with the required expertise to cope with the fixes that Oracle were able to make. In October 2000 the Finance Director who had taken charge of the project also became ill. Over the next few months responsibility for the project fell on the shoulders of a number of individuals: the Acting Director of MISD; the Interim Director of MISD; and the Acting Finance Director. The last of these asked Oracle to assess what was needed to put the system on a sound footing. Oracle concluded that at least 11 people would be needed for a further six months in order to deal with the critical system issues and stabilize the situation. About a quarter of this resource was secured and, as a result, significant improvements took place over the period October 2000 to February 2001.

After the project

The CAPSA steering committee held its final meeting in December 2000. CAPSA was no longer deemed to be an implementation project and its name was changed to Cambridge University Financial System (CUFS). A permanent operations team was established and the support arrangements were substantially improved. In February 2001 an Operations Manager was appointed to take charge of CUFS and a committee, the Financial Systems Management Committee, was set up to oversee it.

Finkelstein concludes his report with a section entitled 'Living with CAPSA'. He starts it thus (para. 10.1):

> CUFS is still not performing acceptably. It is fragile with significant risk of
> failure in handling day-to-day operations. Usability remains poor, workflows

are clumsy with many simple operations requiring multiple screens. Reporting is particularly bad with inadequate and poorly structured reports that are difficult to interpret. Flaws remain in security. System response time is still patchy and frequently impedes progress. Down time is greater than that appropriate for a mission critical enterprise system. At the time of writing the year end procedures have entailed significant disruption. There is a general and warranted lack of confidence in the accuracy of the financial information maintained by CUFS. The research grants module is only marginally fit for purpose. The broad experience of University staff remains that CUFS is a 'sponge' which soaks up time and effort that are not matched by what it produces.

However, he does balance this with grounds for optimism, which include:

System stability has increased substantially since go-live and the magnitude and complexity of the outstanding issues have decreased. The situation is no longer chaotic and there is a good basis for moving forwards. (para. 10.4)

Though new versions and the addition of functionality may destabilise the system in the short term, in the longer term the University can expect some further improvement in terms of stability and 'system quality'. . . . Indeed the latest versions of Oracle Financials may actually deliver in a reasonable form the functionality that Oracle 'sold' to the University. (para. 10.5)

Six months after the two reports were published the Board of Scrutiny once again reported on CAPSA. In this report the Board rehearsed the purpose of CAPSA as set out in 1999 and questioned whether CAPSA's performance was measuring up to its promise. In considering this question it was able to point to a number of ongoing problems, such as the poor quality of the financial reports it produces, its continued unreliability, and its inability to deliver some of the core features expected of it. One sentence, however, stands out in the report, almost as an epitaph to the project:

If CUFS is now working, and it is certainly working much better than it was, it would still be an exaggeration to say that it is working well.

(Report of the Board of Scrutiny on CAPSA, 2002, para. 7)

References

Finkelstein, A. (2001) CAPSA and its implementation, Report to the Audit Committee and the Board of Scrutiny. *Cambridge University Reporter*, Vol. CXXXII, no. 6.

Report of the Board of Scrutiny on CAPSA (2002) *Cambridge University Reporter*, Vol. CXXXII, no. 30.

Shattock, M. (2001) Review of University management and governance issues arising out of the CAPSA project. *Cambridge University Reporter*, Vol. CXXXII, no. 6.

Chapter 6

THE SYSTEMS FAILURES APPROACH PART 1: FROM SITUATION TO SYSTEM

Introduction

Chapter 4 introduced a range of systems concepts and looked at ways in which they can be used to gain insights into IS failures. This and the following chapter will show how these concepts are drawn together to form the Systems Failures Approach. The CAPSA case study in the previous chapter will be used as a source of examples, but because the purpose of this chapter and the next is to develop the approach and show how it works, no attempt is made to provide a full analysis of the CAPSA project.

Many methods and approaches for examining the real world with a view to intervention can be considered to have the stages of abstraction, modelling, manipulation and evaluation. In simple terms, the analysts decide which parts of the real world they are going to consider; they model them in some way, perhaps mathematically or verbally; then they manipulate that model in order to obtain greater understanding, and, in some situations, designs for different formulations. Then having undertaken the modelling they return to 'reality' to compare the results of the previous stages and, if appropriate, decide upon or recommend or facilitate action. Figure 6.1 shows this classic cycle in diagrammatical form.

The concept of 'system' that is central to the Systems Failures Approach – abstract notions of wholes are used as devices through which understanding of real-world information systems is achieved – was introduced in Chapter 4. The goal of the Approach is a systemic interpretation of a failure or potential failure and its context which could, in turn, lead to some action to remedy or prevent. The abstraction is achieved by considering a situation and using a variety of diagrammatic techniques to depict it in a way that improves the initial understanding and enables conceptualization of the

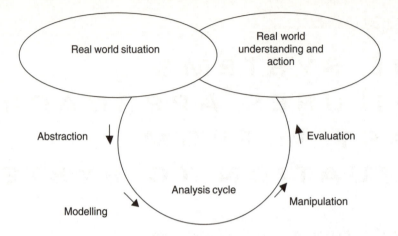

Figure 6.1   The analysis cycle

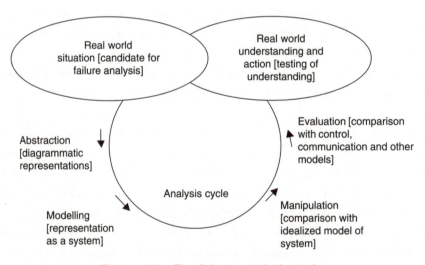

Figure 6.2   The failures analysis cycle

system or systems that can be said to lie at the core of the failure. This system is then modelled, in this case being described in the format of a stereotypical system. This formulation of the real world as a system is then manipulated by comparing it with an idealized model of a system. The results of this comparison may provide sufficient insight or they might identify the need for further comparisons at different hierarchical levels or further investigation of the scene. Figure 6.2 maps the Approach on to the analytical cycle in Figure 6.1.

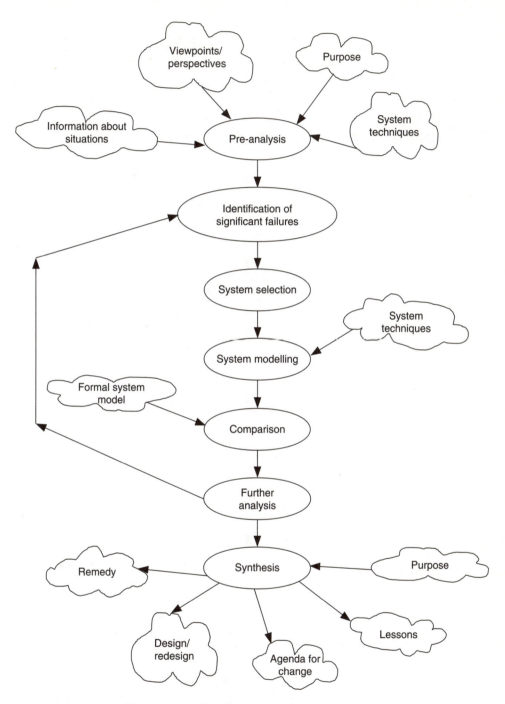

Figure 6.3   The Systems Failures Approach

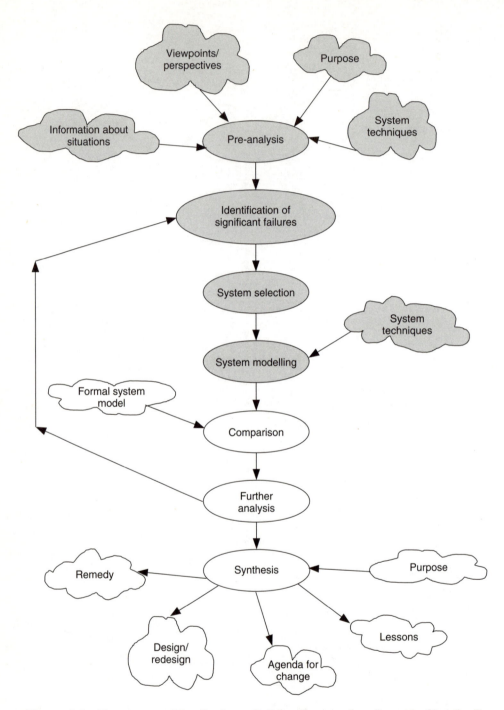

Figure 6.4   The stages of the Systems Failures Approach covered in Chapter 6

At its heart, the Systems Failures Approach has therefore two key features: conceptualization and modelling of the failure situation as a system(s); and comparison of that system(s) with a model of a robust system that is capable of purposeful activity without failure in order to reveal lessons about the failure(s). Its full diagrammatic representation is shown in Figure 6.3.

The stages of the Approach covered in this chapter are highlighted in Figure 6.4.

Pre-Analysis

The first task is to decide which aspects of a situation are being regarded as the failure(s), and hence the focus of the application of the Approach, and which of the many systems that could be conceptualized are likely to advance understanding. This task requires the purpose of the study, and the different viewpoints and perspectives that must be taken into account, to be specified and information about the situation and its history to be gathered and brought together. This early work is called the pre-analysis.

In the CAPSA case, for example, the Council might have commissioned a study to enable it to understand why it was not recognized at an earlier stage that the Chart of Accounts would need to be redeveloped. For such a study the perspectives and viewpoints of the CAPSA Steering Committee would be of primary importance. However, if the Council commissioned a study of the implementation process, then many more viewpoints and perspectives would have to be taken into account. The fewer the viewpoints and perspectives, the more partial the picture, so a four-way balancing act is always necessary between the requirement to be holistic, which underpins systems work, the purpose of the study, the time and cost constraints imposed by the client, and the need for the investigation to be manageable. Level of analysis also becomes important here and forms a bridge between purpose and the many different ways of structuring the situation into systems and, by implication, wider systems, subsystems, sub-subsystems and so on. Thus the study concerning the Chart of Accounts might operate at the account coding level, and disregard staff training and software installations, but an investigation into the adequacies of the implementation plan would need to incorporate all of these aspects as subsystems within a much bigger system, or as a series of nested systems.

For that strand of pre-analysis which is concerned with the gathering and organization of information about the failure situation, a wide variety of techniques are available. These include: spray diagrams; relationship diagrams; multiple-cause diagrams; rich pictures; and non-diagrammatic methods such as lists, databases, charts, etc. The decision about which techniques to use in the pre-analysis of any particular failure rests with the people carrying out the study, but there is one important rule: *the situation must not yet be represented in terms of systems.*

Diagrams of various sorts play a big part in the Approach. During the pre-analysis stage they allow information to be organized and stored and provide working tools for checking that all aspects of the situation are considered and for generating options. They allow experimentation with different boundaries and configurations when systems are being conceptualized and, later in the analysis when systems are being represented and modelled, they provide a means of showing not only structure and process but also interconnectedness. In trying to learn about failures the interactions between the system and the environment, between subsystems and between components within subsystems, are at least as important as the components and subsystems themselves. Because diagrams are so useful they will be considered at some length in this chapter, starting with those that can be used during the pre-analysis stage.

The descriptions of diagram types given here are based on a series of rules and guidelines originally developed within the Systems Discipline of The Open University in the 1980s. They stem from considerable experience of using systems diagrams and of trying to pass on to students the necessary skills to draw them and interpret them. The development of a common approach to diagramming is regarded by some as overly prescriptive, but having clearly defined conventions makes it easier for groups of people to work together on diagrams, and for those groups to be more easily understood by others with whom they might wish to share ideas.

Spray diagrams

A spray diagram is used to record ideas about relationships in the very early stages of analysis, often as a preliminary to drawing a relationship diagram or a multiple-cause diagram. Figure 6.5 shows a spray diagram centred on Cambridge University's need to update their computerized accounting systems to incorporate commitment accounting. The diagram includes both the attempted in-house development and the implementation of the off-the-shelf software. It shows one interpretation of the way various factors

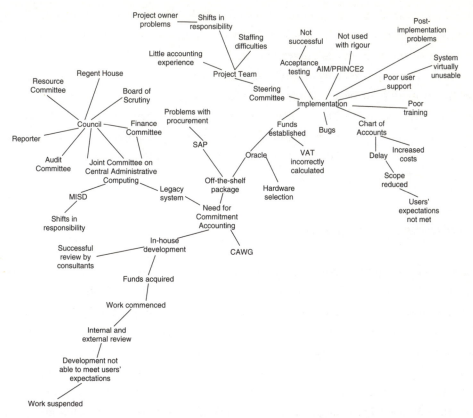

Figure 6.5 Spray diagram – the CAPSA project, including the attempted in-house development

came together to play a part in features of the situation, such as the implementation problems and the difficulties caused by the Chart of Accounts, and either looks at them in greater detail or traces them back through chains of events and to the different committees involved. The amount of detail included in Figure 6.5 has been limited deliberately in order to make its structure clearer, but as a working tool it would be added to and revised as the information gathering proceeded, until it contained all the key pieces of information. For example 'post-implementation problems' could be further subdivided.

Rich pictures

'Rich picture' is a term that was first associated with Checkland's soft systems methodology (SSM; Checkland, 1972). Some interpret the term 'rich picture' literally, specifying that it must be a physical picture, while others consider it to refer to an abstract understanding of a problem situation (see Lewis, 1992). Taking the abstract meaning of the term in the context of the Systems Failures Approach, the whole of the output of the pre-analysis could be said to be a rich picture. Interpreted as a picture or diagram it becomes one of the tools that can be used during pre-analysis. A diagrammatic rich picture seeks to get onto one sheet of paper all of the salient features of a situation in a way that is insightful and can be easily assimilated. It is common to use cartoon-like encapsulations of key ideas or pieces of information, as shown in the example in Figure 6.6.

Relationship diagrams

Relationship diagrams provide snapshots of situations. Lines are drawn to connect components that are significantly related in some way. Although the nature of the relationships included are not specified, different lengths of line can be used to imply different degrees of closeness, although this is sometimes difficult to accommodate on the page in practice. An example is shown in Figure 6.7. When trying to structure a situation as a prelude to conceptualizing systems within it, clusters of components on relationship diagrams may suggest where system or subsystem boundaries could usefully be drawn. For example, Figure 6.7 could give rise to the two possible groupings denoted by dotted lines in Figure 6.8.

Multiple-cause diagrams

Multiple-cause diagrams explore why a given event happened or why a certain class of events tends to occur. They are not intended to predict behaviour, but may be used to develop a list of factors to bear in mind when considering comparable circumstances in the future. Construction normally begins at a single factor/event which is then traced backwards. In Figure 6.9 the starting factor is user dissatisfaction with CUFS.

The elements of the diagram are phrases and arrows. The phrases may be names of 'things', with or without their relevant associated variables, or events. The arrows may represent causes or may mean 'contributes to', 'is followed by', 'enables', or something similar. Unless annotation indicates otherwise, no distinction is drawn between necessary and/or sufficient causes.

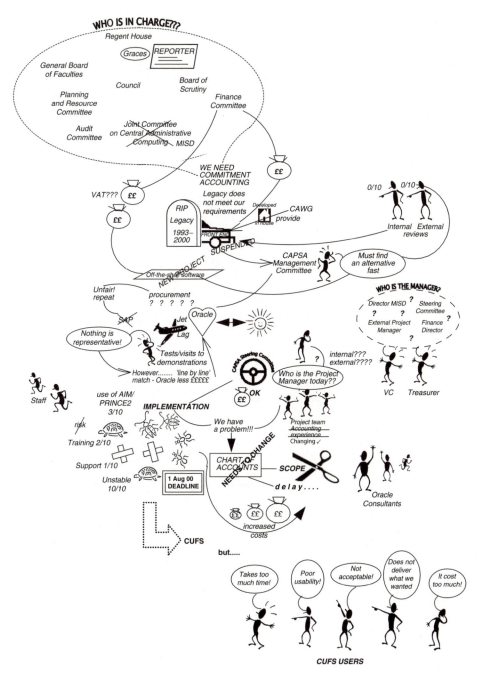

Figure 6.6   Rich picture – the CAPSA project

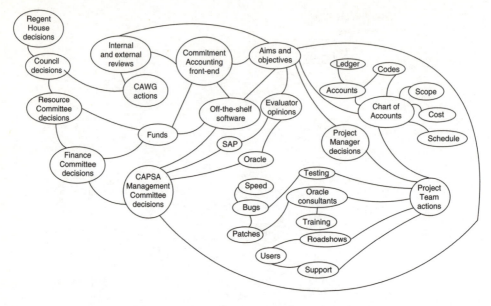

Figure 6.7   Relationship diagram – the CAPSA project

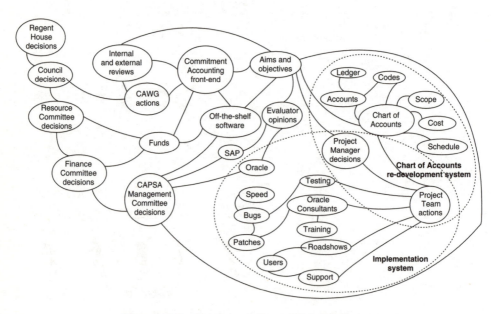

Figure 6.8   Experimenting with boundaries

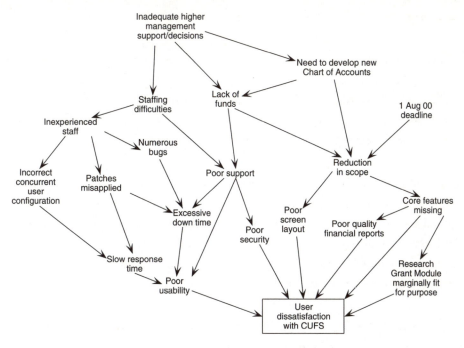

Figure 6.9   Multiple-cause diagram – user dissatisfaction with CUFS

Identifying Significant Failures and Selecting a System

Chapter 2 discussed the notion of failure and argued that the extent to which something can be judged a failure must depend upon the standpoint from which it is viewed. It also presented the idea of failures being regarded as the outputs, or lack of outputs, of the transformation processes being carried out within systems. These ideas are combined in the next stage of the Systems Failures Approach where all aspects of the pre-analysis are brought together to identify the focus for the analysis and specify the systems from which the failure(s) can be said to have emerged.

The situation will already have been labelled a failure or a potential failure in general terms, otherwise the Approach would not need to used, but now it is necessary to move towards a more specific statement of the focus of the analysis. (The words 'move towards' have been chosen carefully to try to reflect the uncertainties of defini-tion – uncertainties that are inevitable given the nature of the concept of failure – and the need for iteration, which this approach shares with most other systems approaches.)

A number of serious concerns were raised in Chapter 5:

1. The new on-line commitment accounting system cost significantly more than had initially been envisaged.
2. The system failed to meet all of the requirements set for it.
3. Implementation led to significant disruption to the working of the University to the point where the integrity of its accounting was compromised.

These could, in combination or separately, be regarded as 'the failures'. A different, narrower, view of the situation might be that the inability to foresee the changes required to the Chart of Accounts constituted the significant failure. Another view might consider that reduced functionality was the significant failure, and that although the changes required to the Chart of Accounts could be said to have triggered this failure, it was not actually part of it.

Another way of looking at the CAPSA project would be to separate it into distinct phases, each containing an apparently significant failure:

1. The in-house development
2. The chart of accounts redevelopment
3. The implementation.

But each of these could also be broken down further if it was thought necessary to focus more narrowly, with a view, perhaps, to generating generic lessons that could be applied to a whole range of projects. Within the third, for example, staffing difficulties, ineffective training and ineffective use of project management methodologies, could each be regarded as the subject for widespread concern and thus a useful subject for analysis in its own right.

Faced with ranges of options such as this, people using the Approach have no hard and fast rules to tell them where to begin; a judgement has to be made. This judgement has to be based on purpose, viewpoint and perspective, but there are no objective criteria for it. The concept of 'top event' which dictates the starting point for a fault tree analysis has no equivalent in this approach. Even after embarking upon an analysis it may become necessary to widen the scope or narrow it, or to switch between levels, but again this will be based on subjective judgement.

A whole range of systems relevant to the failures could be conceptualized from within the CAPSA project. These include:

- an on-line commitment accounting system
- an in-house software development system
- a procurement system
- an implementation system
- a chart of accounts redevelopment system
- a staff training system
- a risk assessment system
- a user support system
- a project management system.

Within the Approach, failure is regarded as an output, or lack of outputs, of transformation processes carried out by a system. By putting trial systems boundaries around aspects of the situation, and experimenting with various configurations, permutations and combinations, it should be possible to delineate a notional system that carried out, or was supposed to carry out, those transformations. Most importantly, the system which is conceptualized must also appear to be a likely candidate to take the analysis forward. It is probable that because of the complexity of the situation the analysis will have to be conducted at a number of levels within any system. It may also be necessary to select a number of interacting systems and carry them all forward through the subsequent comparison process, scrutinizing them individually, and as a whole. Considerable care is needed at this stage since splitting a failure into different phases or different aspects could inhibit a full investigation without this notion of interacting systems. Important interrelationships might be lost and the analysis cease to be holistic.

The system(s) that have been selected need to be modelled in some detail. This process is described in the next section, which uses the authors' conceptualization of the implementation system as an example.

Modelling Systems

Models of any systems used in the analysis have to be sufficiently detailed to enable switching between levels to be carried out and to allow structure and process to be represented in the formats necessary for comparison. (Comparison is dealt with in the next chapter.) As a minimum, this requires:

1. Name and definition of the system(s)
2. Description of the components of the system(s)
3. Description of the components and relationships in the environment of each system
4. Identification of the wider system
5. Description of the inputs and outputs
6. Identification of the system(s) variables
7. The structural relationships between components to be established
8. Some indication of the relationships between the variables that describe the behaviour of the system(s).

For example, the components of the implementation system might be said to include:

- The Oracle consultants
- The project management team
- The project management methodologies used
- The Chart of Accounts
- The installation of software subsystem(s)
- The staff training subsystem(s).

Within the environment the following might be identified:

- Cambridge University staff (the users of the system)
- The University Governance system
- The independent consultants
- The Legacy system.

Important variables might be: the number of people working on the implementation; the level of commitment of the project team; the number of software patches required; and so on.

Systems diagrams, particularly input–output diagrams, systems maps and influence diagrams are the main modelling tools at this point in the Approach.

Input–output diagrams

An input–output diagram is a simple form of flow block diagram with the system represented by a single box, and inputs and outputs shown as labelled arrows. For an

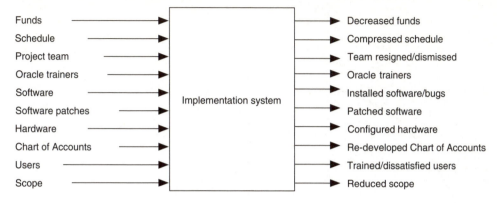

Figure 6.10   Input-output diagram – the implementation system

example, see Figure 6.10. Although this diagrammatic form is very simple, it is a very effective way of showing what the system would or should do – that is, take inputs and transform them into outputs.

Systems maps

A systems map is essentially a snapshot showing the components of a system and its environment at a point in time. Primarily it shows structure, but the positioning of components provides some information about the relative strengths of relationships. The only elements allowed are named components; linking lines, arrows, etc., are not permitted.

Within the Systems Failures Approach, systems maps are very useful when experimenting with trial boundaries, for communicating to others the structure of the system being used, and for determining the levels at which the analysis should be conducted. Figure 6.11 shows a map of the implementation system outlined earlier. The boundary of the system encloses the subsystems and elements that comprise its components and separates them from the components that make up its environment.

Influence diagrams

An influence diagram is also a snapshot based on structure, but its prime purpose is to explore relationships. It is often the case that closer examination of interactions, perhaps also using a matrix of interactions, leads to a redefinition of the system or a regrouping of its components.

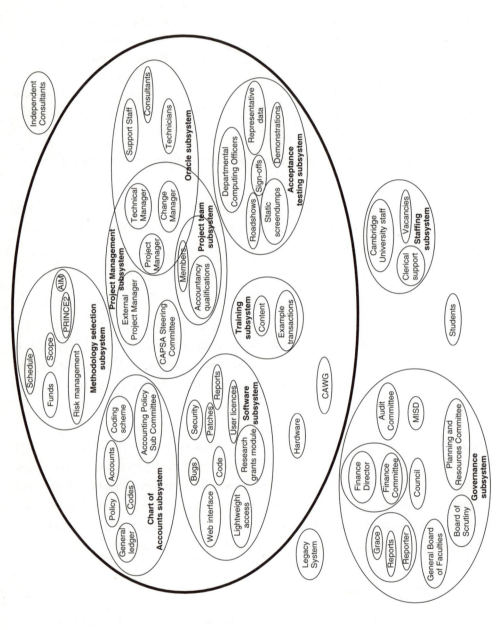

Figure 6.11   Systems map – the implementation system

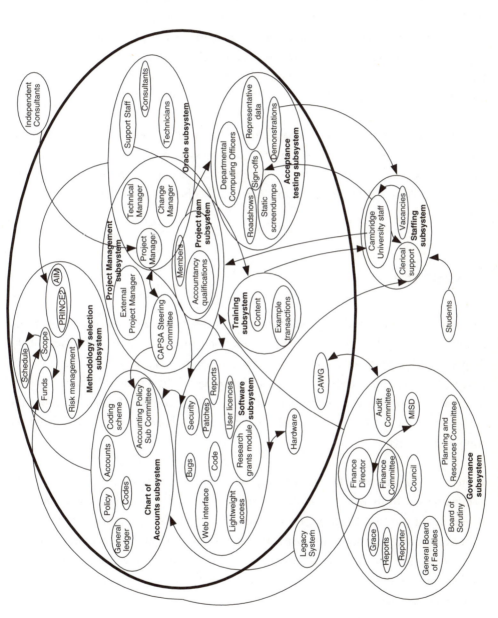

Figure 6.12   Influence diagram – the implementation system

The elements of an influence diagram are named components and arrows. The arrows may be labelled to distinguish between different types of influence, such as influence via finance, information, statutory regulation and so on, and a variation in the thickness of the lines is used to indicate different strengths of influence. As in systems maps, space and relative distance reveal information about the nature of the relationships shown; thus, for example, a component that is shown as important in terms of its degree of influence could, from its position, also be seen to be isolated and remote.

An influence diagram of the implementation system is shown in Figure 6.12. A one-way arrow, such as that joining the Legacy system to the Chart of Accounts subsystem, shows that the former can or does influence the latter, but the latter has no significant influence over the former. Double-headed arrows denote two-way influences.

Summary

The activity of conceptualizing and modelling systems as a prelude to studying a failure situation can itself be likened to a transformation process. It begins with users of the Approach being confronted with a situation that someone has identified as a failure or potential failure and ends with sufficient knowledge of the situation in systems terms to be able to represent it, or aspects of it, in the appropriate format to allow the comparison stage of the Systems Failures Approach to begin. It is achieved using the following process:

- *Stage 1: Pre-analysis*   Define the purpose of the analysis and the viewpoints and perspectives from which it is being carried out. Gather together source material and investigate the situation, examining it from the various viewpoints that have been identified as important. Organize the information into forms that will render it usable. This may involve the use of rich pictures, spray diagrams, multiple-cause diagrams, databases, and so on. Exact methods for pre-analysis are not prescribed, but systems analyses are proscribed.
- *Stage 2: Identify significant failure(s) and select system(s)*   The situation itself will have already been labelled a failure or potential failure in general terms, but now the failure(s) must be specified more precisely in accordance with the outcomes of the pre-analysis. Use trial boundaries to structure relevant aspects of the situation into a

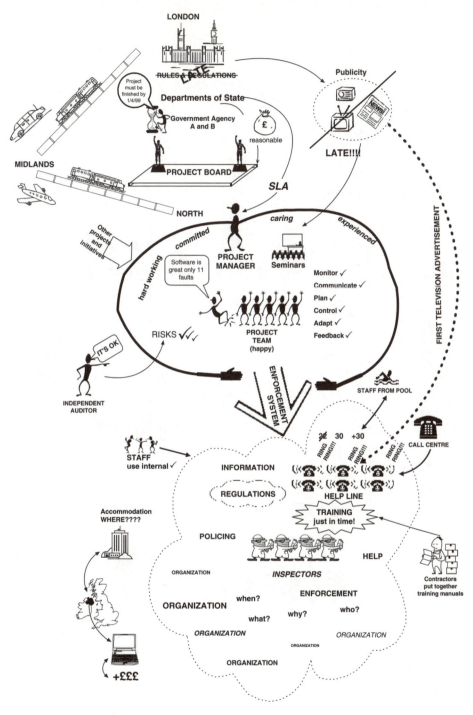

Figure 6.13 Rich picture – Project A

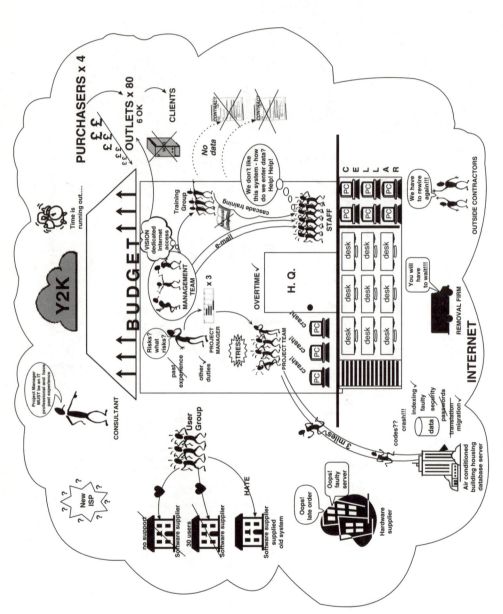

Figure 6.14   Rich picture – Project B

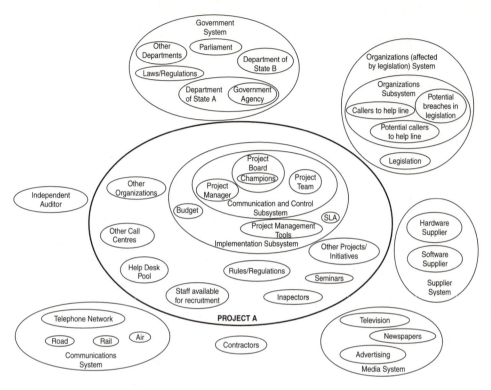

Figure 6.15   Systems map – Project A

range of systems and select the system(s) to be carried forward to the next stage. For the purposes of analysis, the significant failure(s) will be regarded as the outputs of the system(s).

- *Stage 3: Model the system(s)*   Clarify the nature of the system(s) using a set of systems questions and build diagrammatic models of structure and process as a precursor to representing various aspects of the system(s) and its behaviour, possibly at different levels, in the formats required for comparison.

This chapter has introduced a range of diagrams that may play a part in these three stages. Further illustrations of some of the key rich pictures and systems maps are shown in Figures 6.13-6.16. They relate to the two projects that were described in Chapter 3.

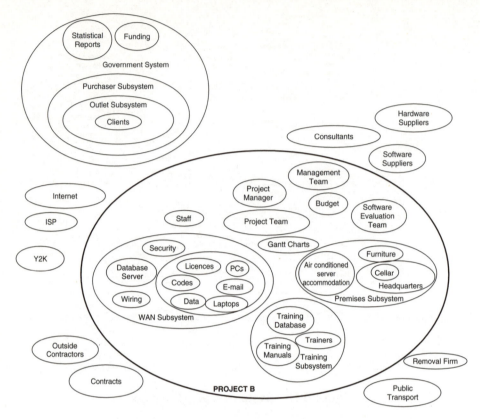

Figure 6.16   Systems map – Project B

References

Checkland, P.B. (1972) Towards a systems-based methodology for real world problem solving. *Journal of Systems Engineering*, 3: 87–116.

Lewis, P.J. (1992) Rich picture building in the soft systems methodology. *European journal of Information Systems*, 1: 351–360.

Chapter 7

THE SYSTEMS FAILURES APPROACH PART 2: COMPARISON AND SYNTHESIS

Introduction

Chapter 6 was concerned with the first of the two key features of the Systems Failures Approach: conceptualization and modelling of the failure situation as a system(s). This chapter looks at the second: comparison of that system(s) with a model of a robust system which is capable of purposeful activity without failure, and synthesis of the results to reveal lessons about the failure(s). The stages of the Approach covered in this chapter are highlighted in Figure 7.1.

The Formal System Model

As was shown in Chapter 4, systems concepts provide a means of achieving understanding that would not otherwise be available. However, trying to achieve understanding of a complex situation through the use of individual concepts can be a somewhat haphazard process. Not only will the outcomes be dependent on the choice of concepts, but the study as a whole will, in effect, risk losing its systemic property by failing to be systematic.

To avoid these shortcomings the Systems Failures Approach uses a model that unites most system concepts. This model is called the Formal System Model (FSM). It is adapted from Checkland (1981), who in turn drew on the ideas of Churchman (1971, pp. 42–78), particularly his concept of a teleological system, and Jenkins (1969).

The term 'formal' is used in the title to convey the provision of a form or structural framework into which something can be fitted. The bare bones of the framework are

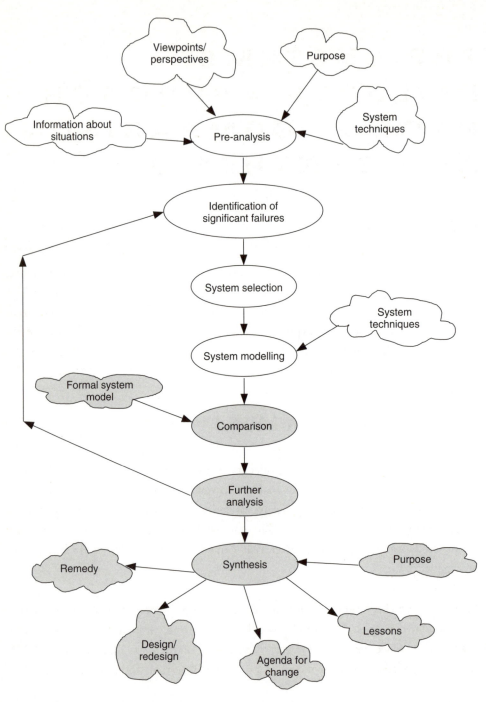

Figure 7.1   The stages of the Systems Failures Approach covered in Chapter 7

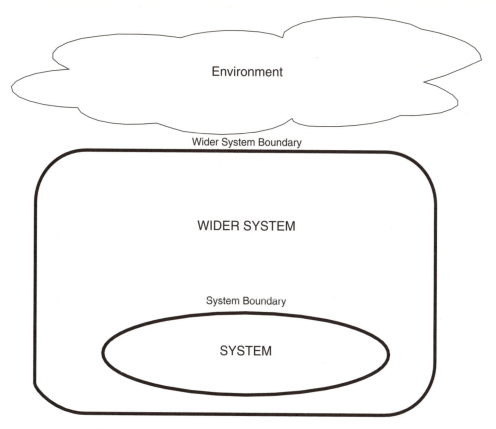

Figure 7.2   System, wider system and environment

shown in Figure 7.2. These are: a system (the Formal System); a wider system; and an environment. The concept of environment is exactly the same as the one introduced in Chapter 4 and as depicted beyond the system boundary in systems maps and influence diagrams in the previous chapter. It is only represented slightly differently here to make the model clearer.

As can be seen in Figure 7.2, the wider system represents the next hierarchical level upwards from the system. It affects the system in a number of ways. It defines its purpose and sets its objectives. It influences the decision-takers within the system and monitors the performance of the system as a whole. It also provides the resources that the system needs in order to function. The environment disturbs the system directly but it also disturbs it indirectly through the wider system. Similarly, the system attempts to influence the environment both directly and via its wider system. These relationships are summarized in Figure 7.3.

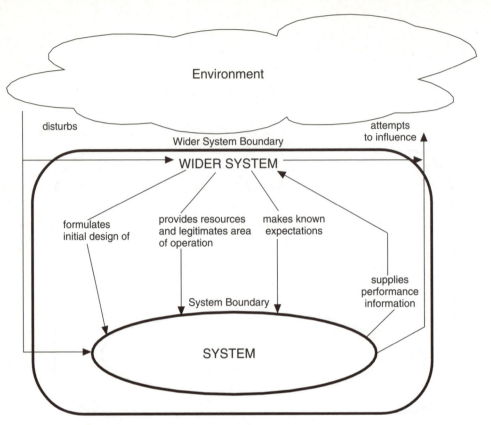

Figure 7.3 Relationships between the system, the wider system and the environment

Although a powerful wider system might constrain the activities of a system by defining goals and exercising control, and only providing those resources that are necessary to achieve those goals, it can also enhance the authority of the system. If the legitimacy of the objectives and activities of the wider system have been established, this legitimacy can be extended to justify the activities of the system and its subsystems.

The Formal System comprises a decision-making subsystem, a performance-monitoring subsystem and a set of subsystems and elements that carry out the tasks of the system and thus effect its transformations by converting inputs into outputs. The decision-making subsystem manages the system. It is responsible for decisions about how the purposes of the system are to be achieved – such as, which transformations are to be carried out and by what means – and for providing the resources to enable this to happen. It makes known its expectations to the subsystems and components that

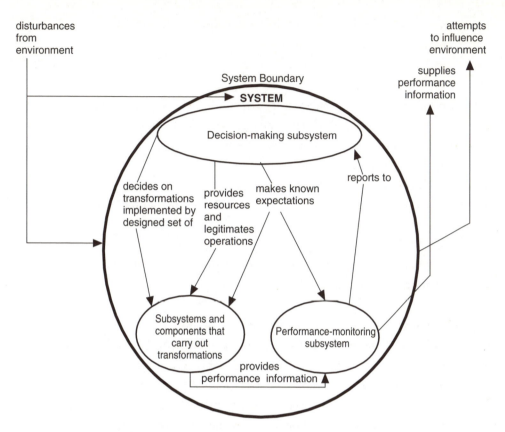

Figure 7.4   Relationships between subsystems

carry out the system's transformations and to the performance-monitoring subsystem. It is therefore the decision-making subsystem that allows the system to exhibit choice, and thus behave as a purposeful system. The performance-monitoring subsystem is charged with observing the transformation processes and reporting deviations from the expectations to the decision-making subsystem so that it can initiate corrective action where necessary. These three subsystems, and the relationships between them, are shown in Figure 7.4.

An equivalent relationship to that between a wider system and a system can be said to exist between the Formal System and its subsystems. A Formal System, by definition, has requirements of its subsystems, but such relationships need not preclude each subsystem having a certain amount of autonomy in deciding how those expectations are met.

The comprehensive representation of the Formal System Model is shown in Figure 7.5. Its features can be summarized as follows:

- a decision-making subsystem
- a performance-monitoring subsystem
- a set of subsystems and elements that carry out the tasks of the system and thus effect its transformations by converting inputs into outputs
- a degree of connectivity between the components
- an environment with which the system interacts
- boundaries separating the system from its wider system and the wider system from the environment
- resources
- a continuous purpose or mission that gives rise to the expectations
- some guarantee of continuity.

Control, which was introduced in Chapter 4, is most obviously seen in relation to the workings of the performance-monitoring subsystem. Performance monitoring generates the information required in order to exercise control. Control can then be used to minimize, as far as possible, the deviations of the outputs of the system from the values that will enable the expectations to be met. The main forces behind the need for control are the disturbances coming from the environment. Chapter 4 set out a number of preconditions that need to be met if control is to be successfully established and consistently maintained. This list of conditions can be used to investigate control problems more fully.

Communication is another concept that occupies a central role in the Formal System Model. In addition to the communication aspects of control, the following are highlighted:

1. Communication between the system and its environment.
2. The flow of information from the wider system, via the system, to the subsystems, and vice versa.
3. Numerous communication links within the system and the subsystems.

Part of the reason for comparing systems representations with the FSM is to reveal whether any of these communication links are missing, or inadequate, or simply not used.

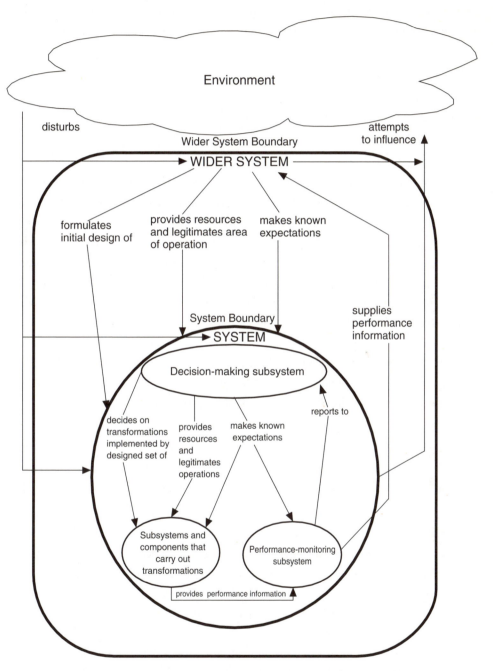

Figure 7.5   The Formal System Model (from Fortune, 1993)

Insights gained from comparison between the FSM and the system conceptualized from a failure situation will be found within subsystems, in the links between subsystems, or be associated with one or more of the following interfaces between boundaries:

- environment–wider system
- environment–system
- wider system–system
- interfaces between subsystems.

Because of the hierarchical nature of the FSM each of its subsystems can also be perceived as a Formal System with its own decision-making, performance-monitoring and transformation-effecting components, and each one of those could then, in turn, also be regarded as a Formal System, and so on, until the level was reached where the components must or need only be regarded as elements or the system becomes purposive rather than purposeful. This notion of hierarchy is a very important aspect of the Approach. Unless it is taken on board and applied it is difficult to avoid the charge that the model is a unitarist one that ignores concepts such as conflict and power. The decision-making subsystem is itself just that – a subsystem. It may, at one extreme, be made up of people who share a single world view and are united in some common purpose, or it could be a changing balance of forces or disparate groups who are making temporary alliances as they jockey for position.

Wide experience (see Peters & Fortune, 1992) of comparing systems representations of failure situations with the FSM has shown there to be recurring themes which emerge from such comparisons. The following are typical points of difference:

1. Deficiencies in the apparent organizational structure of the system, such as a lack of either a performance-measuring subsystem or a control/decision-making subsystem.
2. No clear statements of purpose supplied in a comprehensible form to the system from the wider system.
3. Deficiencies in the performance of one or more subsystems – for example, the performance-measuring subsystem may not have performed its task adequately.
4. Lack of an effective means of communication between the various subsystems.
5. Inadequate design of one or more subsystems.
6. Not enough consideration given to the influence of the environment, and insufficient resources to cope with those environmental disturbances that were foreseen.

7. An imbalance between the resources applied to the basic transformation processes and those allocated to the related monitoring and control processes, perhaps leading at one extreme to quality problems and, at the other, to cost or output quantity problems.

In order to undertake the process of comparison it is first necessary to represent the system that has been conceptualized in the same format as the FSM. Figure 7.6 provides an example. It shows the implementation system, still as conceptualized in Chapter 6, but now reordered into the format of the FSM.

The next stage is to compare the FSM with the system that has been conceptualized. This process identifies discrepancies and reveals gaps in one's understanding of the situation. In the case of the CAPSA implementation system, comparison with the FSM shows many areas where there appear to be discrepancies. One arises at the interface between the environment and the system. Severe technical and financial problems resulted from the disturbances caused by the incorrect assumption that Legacy's Chart of Accounts coding scheme would be unchanged in the new system. Another example is the system's inability to influence the environment to a sufficient extent. This is one of the explanations for the failure of those in charge of the project to gain the support of the future users of the system.

A further area of interest to emerge from the comparison involves the relationship between the wider system and the system. There is evidence to suggest that the wider system failed to formulate an effective plan. The project plan had to be changed to a substantial extent on two occasions. The first of these was in order to accommodate the need to redevelop the Chart of Accounts, and the second was to ensure that the project was completed on time by replacing the original phased implementation with a 'big bang' approach and by reducing the scope of the project. The comparison also suggests that an effective communications and control plan was not developed. The principal officers of the University failed to involve themselves with many of the accounting policy issues and made decisions without informing the Project Manager.

Overall, the implementation system gives an impression that the project was not managed as a whole. This is reflected in poor decisions and inadequate control, both of which are illuminated further when considering the relevant subsystems. The comparison indicates clearly that the decision-making subsystem was deficient. Responsibility for the project fell on numerous shoulders, on one occasion without the post-holder's

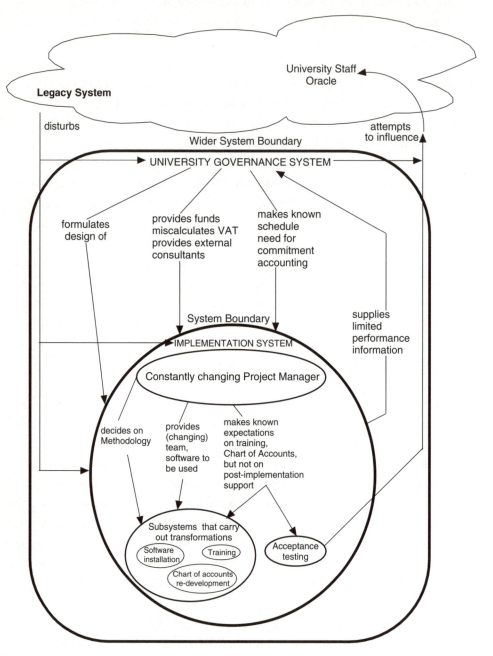

Figure 7.6 The implementation system in the format of the FSM

apparent knowledge or agreement. Outside consultants were used extensively in the decision-making process, leading to a conflict of interest, internal tensions and low morale. The performance-monitoring subsystem seems to be missing almost entirely. Indeed, the lack of control, feedback and effective communication channels were all mentioned in the report. An independent review of the project criticized the project's control systems and drew attention to the lack of progress and rising costs. A further report highlighted the project's ineffective financial-monitoring, record-keeping and communications.

The comparison also indicates that a number of the subsystems that carried out the transformations were inadequately designed. The training subsystem was not effective. The training was carried out by external consultants and suffered from numerous problems, including content insufficiently related to the work of the University and many example transactions being unrepresentative. The software installation subsystem was also deficient. The software threw up a substantial number of bugs and many software patches were dropped or misapplied.

These and other discrepancies revealed by the comparison between Figure 7.6 and the FSM are further explored in Table 7.1.

Figures 7.7 and 7.8 show Project A and Project B, respectively, modelled in the format of the Formal System Model. Comparison between Figure 7.7 and the FSM reveals the discrepancies shown in Table 7.2. The discrepancies for Project B are shown in Table 7.3

In order to generate sufficient understanding it is usually necessary to make further comparisons against the FSM at different hierarchical levels. These can be upwards and/or downwards. When moving up, the system that has just been considered will next be viewed as a subsystem of a higher-level system. Moving down a level, what was regarded as a subsystem will be perceived as the system. Judgement about whether a change in level is appropriate, and if so whether it should be up to a wider system or down to what was a subsystem, will need to take account of the nature of the system(s) as conceptualized earlier in the Approach and the results of the first comparison. Switches such as these between different hierarchical levels will be seen in Chapter 9.

It is possible that, in the extreme case, a situation that was designed to match the model precisely, and should thus be capable of operating without failure, could still be judged by some observers to be a failure if, for example, they regarded it as unethical or believed that

Table 7.1 Discrepancies revealed by comparison between Figure 7.6 and the FSM

Aspect of the FSM	Discrepancy or Comments
Environment	Both the wider system and the system failed to consider environmental influences adequately because the implementation plan was based on the incorrect assumption that the Legacy Chart of Accounts coding scheme would be unchanged in the new system. Although the comparison suggests that the wider system and the system made an attempt to influence the environment, for example by gaining staff acceptance for the project, this was not successful.
Formulates initial design/decides on transformations	Although the wider system set out an implementation plan this was changed twice so that the phased implementation and gradual roll-out of the original plan was abandoned and replaced with a 'big-bang' approach. Furthermore, there is little evidence to suggest that clear measures of performance were devised or that an effective communications plan was developed. The system decided on the use of two implementation methodologies but there is evidence to suggest that they were never properly established or used with rigour; furthermore, at the system level there is once again little evidence to suggest that measures of performance were formulated and there is no indication of a clear communications plan.
Provides resources and legitimates area of operation	The wider system provided the necessary funds but miscalculated the VAT. They also provided external consultants to help oversee the project and a management team that was substantially changed on two occasions. The system provided a project team but most of the team were not qualified accounts. A number of the team members took early retirement or resigned and these were replaced by external

Table 7.1 (*Continued*)

Aspect of the FSM	Discrepancy or Comments
	consultants leading to tensions and conflict. Although the system successfully selected a software supplier, this led to controversy as the procurement process breached EU regulations and had to be repeated.
Makes known expectations	The wider system set out a schedule; however their reluctance to change the 'go-live' date of the project led to a reduction in its scope. At the system level there were unsuccessful attempts to gain staff commitment and overcome their resistance to change, indeed the roadshow intended to demonstrate CAPSA functionality and capture interest had precisely the reverse effect. Furthermore staff training was undertaken by outside consultants so that the content of the training was insufficiently related to the work of the University. The project team only paid 'lip service' to risk management and did not make their expectations on post-implementation support clear.
Supplies performance information	The system provided limited performance information to the wider system. However there appears to be no evidence of any feedback from the subsystems that carried out the transformations.
Decision-making subsystem	There was no consistent decision-making team in charge of the project because organizational changes within the University shifted responsibility for the project; indeed on many occasions it was unclear who was managing the project. For example, at one point the principal officers of the University expected the newly-appointed Director of MISD actively to manage the project but the Director of MISD believed his deputy was actually in charge. There is evidence that many decisions were made without the knowledge of the decision-making subsystem and that the

Table 7.1   (*Continued*)

Aspect of the FSM	Discrepancy or Comments
	decision-making subsystem failed to view the project as a whole, leading to inadequate decision making and poor control.
Subsystems that carry out transformations	There is evidence to suggest the subsystems that carried out the transformations were not effective. Training was poor, no arrangements were put in place to support users and work on configuring the system threw up a substantial number of bugs.
Performance monitoring subsystem	There is no evidence of an effective performance monitoring subsystem. Financial monitoring did not appear to take place so that the cost of the project nearly doubled; staffing difficulties were not identified and, although acceptance testing was undertaken, the results were unsuccessful.

it breached human rights. Pearce and Fortune (2002) have examined ways of eliminating this possibility. One approach they have suggested is to encompass ethical and human rights considerations within the list of features that need to be present if the components of a situation are to meet the requirements for purposeful action without failure. They felt that this approach would have the benefit of being simple as far as the list of features is concerned, but that it could be problematical. First, it begs the question whether ethical and human rights considerations are genuinely different from other considerations, such as other legislative requirements like data protection, to the point where they cannot be covered by other features on the list. Another reservation is that the list of features may start to become a checklist rather than a distillation of the model itself. Although it is very easy to add words to the list of features, it is very difficult to see how the form of the FSM could be modified to reflect this addition.

Another option they suggested was retaining the existing FSM and regarding ethical concerns, human rights issues and legislation as important components of the environment that are potentially disturbing the wider system and the system. They believed that this would allow ethical and legislative requirements to be considered in

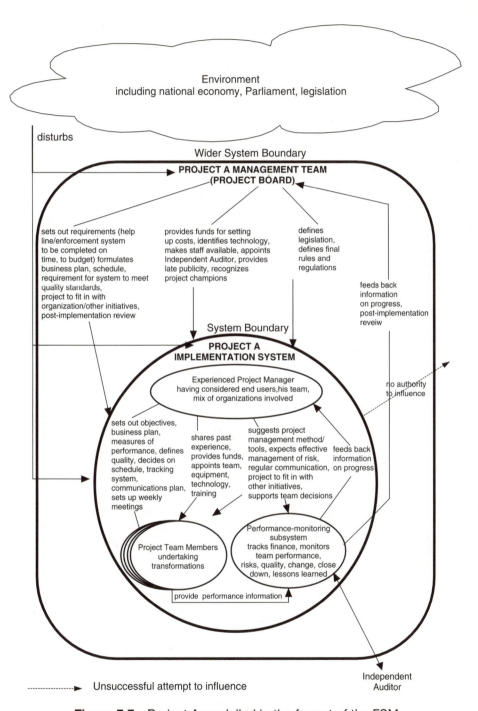

Figure 7.7 Project A modelled in the format of the FSM

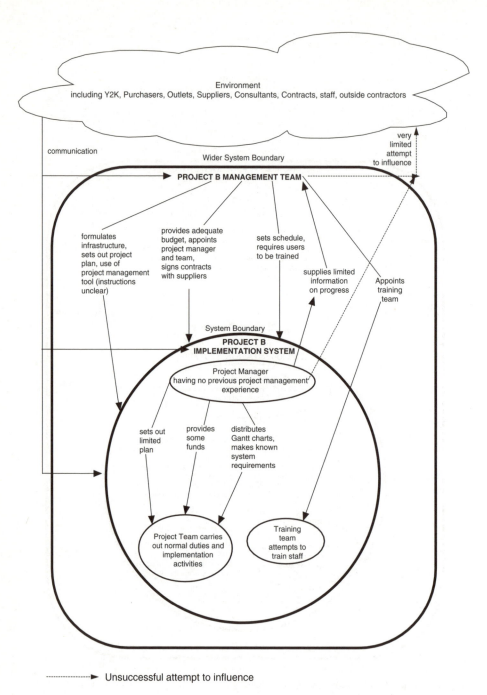

Environment
including Y2K, Purchasers, Outlets, Suppliers, Consultants, Contracts, staff, outside contractors

communication

very
limited
attempt
to influence

Wider System Boundary

PROJECT B MANAGEMENT TEAM

formulates
infrastructure,
sets out project
plan, use of
project management
tool (instructions
unclear)

provides adequate
budget, appoints
project manager
and team,
signs contracts
with suppliers

sets schedule,
requires users
to be trained

supplies limited
information
on progress

Appoints
training
team

System Boundary

**PROJECT B
IMPLEMENTATION SYSTEM**

Project Manager
having no previous project management
experience

sets out
limited
plan

provides
some
funds

distributes
Gantt charts,
makes known
system
requirements

Project Team carries
out normal duties and
implementation
activities

Training
team
attempts to
train staff

┈┈┈┈▶ Unsuccessful attempt to influence

Figure 7.8 Project B modelled in the format of the FSM

Table 7.2 Comparison between Project A and the FSM

Aspect of the FSM	Discrepancies
Environment	Although the Project Board took some account of environmental influences they failed to take sufficient account of certain important aspects such as those arising from the long and protracted nature of decision-making at Government level. There is little evidence to suggest that any effort was made by the wider system to influence its environment in order to prevent delays and ensure publicity was available on time. At the system level there is evidence that disturbances from the environment were considered and efforts made to provide resources to cope with the disturbances. The efforts to mitigate the effects of late publicity are a good example of this. The information gathered suggests that the system appreciated the influence of the political and legal system in the wider system's environment but was not able to influence it.
Formulates initial design/decides on transformations	None detected.
Provides resources	The wider system provided adequate funds but the publicity was delivered late.
Makes known expectations	Though some of the detail was missing, no significant discrepancies detected.
Supplies performance information	None detected.

Table 7.2 (Continued)	
Aspect of the FSM	Discrepancies
Decision-making subsystem	None detected.
Subsystems that carry out transformations	None detected.
Performance-monitoring subsystem	None detected.

analysis to the extent of looking for a reaction to the disturbance, but felt that it may fail to probe to sufficient depths the underlying structure and processes of the wider system and the system. They also feared that it might give a false view of the requirements placed upon the system. According to the FSM, the system responds to disturbances from the environment by trying to influence it. To suggest that ethical issues or human rights requirements are somehow negotiable is to misunderstand their real impact.

A further approach they considered was one that recognizes the need for ethics and human rights to be dynamic features running through a system and encompassed within the 'guarantee of continuity'. They suggested that this could be achieved through examination of the real world situation, seeking confirmation that consideration had been given to such issues or that features that could be interpreted in terms of ethics and human rights were present. In particular, the examination would focus upon the wider system and the decision-making subsystem with the expectation that ethical and human rights issues would be accounted for in the function 'makes known expectations'. It would be right and proper for both the wider system and the decision-making subsystem of the system to ensure that the fundamentals of ethical and human rights requirements are complied with when delivering the system's purpose; therefore, it could be said that through this mechanism ethical and human rights issues transcend decision-making. Equally if a system is to operate in an ethical fashion and take into account human rights, then there would be an expectation that the 'legitimates operations function' would be expected to follow this convention. There is a potential drawback to this approach in that the model incorporates no specific means by which ethical concerns and human rights can be communicated through the wider system and systems expectations. One

Table 7.3 Comparison between Project B and the FSM

Aspect of the FSM	Discrepancies
Environment	The wider system failed to consider environmental influences adequately. For example, although the Management Team adopted some of the recommendations made by the Consultants, they did not appoint an experienced Project Manager. Furthermore, they failed to take account of the needs of the organizations with which they held short-term contracts. There is no evidence to suggest that the disturbances from the environment were considered. Only a very limited attempt was made by the wider system to influence the environment. The Management Team made no attempts to influence suppliers and the wider system made no effort to contact Outlets directly. At the system level the Project Manager's visits to the Outlets were an attempt to influence them but the attempt was unsuccessful.
Formulates initial design/decides on transformations	The wider system did set out a project plan, but failed to devise measures of performance and instructions on the use of project management tools were unclear. At the system level: only a limited plan was devised; the schedule was changed; there was no specified tracking system or measures of performance; and no communications plan was produced.
Provides resources	At the wider system level there was inadequate provision of human resources, there were no Lessons Learned Files, and the technology provided was limited and not fully understood. At the system level the Project Team possessed poor understanding of the technology and were provided with inadequate support.

Table 7.3   (Continued)

Aspect of the FSM	Discrepancies
Makes known expectations	The wider system did not make all their expectations clear and were particularly poor at communicating the reasons for their decisions. At the system level there were no attempts to gain staff commitment or overcome their resistance to change, and the Project Team was not expected to manage risk. Furthermore, staff training was not within the authority of the Project Manager.
Supplies performance information	Only limited feedback on performance occurred between the Project Manager and the Management Team and at the system level there was no evidence of provision of performance information.
Decision-making subsystem	The Project Manager had no previous project management experience.
Subsystems that carry out transformations	The Project Team had to perform their normal duties as well as carry out the transformations. A separate team was instructed directly by the wider system to train staff.
Performance-monitoring subsystem	There was no evidence of a performance-monitoring subsystem and no post-implementation review took place.

way of dealing with this would be to have a supporting set of heuristics that is tailored to the specific situation under consideration. The example provided in Pearce and Fortune (2002, p. 281) relates to the use of criminal intelligence obtained from informants:

Is there interference with someone's rights? *(Operational and subjective decision)*

Is there a positive obligation to take action?

Is the action lawful? *(Is there a law that says I can do this?)*

Is the action necessary? *(Could the same result be achieved by means that did not interfere with someone's rights?)*

Is the action proportionate? *(Is the action unfair or arbitrary? Is it limited to that which is necessary to achieve the aim? How does the proposed action balance the rights of the individual against the community as a whole?)*

Is the action accountable? *(Is there a process for recording decisions and the reasons for them that will stand scrutiny?)*

Iteration and synthesis

Figure 7.1 shows the main iteration loop within the Approach, but many more loops could be shown. At every stage, iteration may be required, both within stages and between them. For instance, the absence of a performance information feedback loop revealed in Figure 7.6 or the almost complete lack of a performance-monitoring sub-system for Project B (see Figure 7.8) may trigger further investigation, pre-analysis and/or modelling. Gaps may appear in the information gathered during the investigation or it may become clear that choices – perhaps relatively minor ones, such as placing a component in the environment rather than in the system at the pre-analysis stage – were inappropriate, thus making it necessary to revisit a particular stage in the Approach. Because multiple viewpoints and perspectives are required, it may even be necessary to make a number of passes through the entire Approach. In the extreme case, a situation that was designed to match the model precisely, and should thus be capable of operating without failure, could still be judged by some observers to be a failure because it relied on a high degree of coercion or encouraged self-exploitation or breaking of the laws governing data protection, for example. The failure would not emerge until their perspectives were considered.

When the analysis begins to look complete, it becomes necessary to draw the threads back together to build an understanding of the failure as a whole. In order to maintain the systemic nature of one's understanding the best way to begin the synthesis is to return once again to the Formal System Model and use the findings from all the iterations to remodel the system at the various key levels.

Once that has been done the format of the remainder of the synthesis may well vary according to the purposes to which the results of the study will be put. As a first stage it may be helpful to prepare another version of the set of FSMs that emphasize the salient features. What is 'salient' is always a difficult judgement, with the answer depending upon the eye of the beholder, but the starting point for determining it will be the viewpoint, perspectives and purpose that informed the pre-analysis.

It may be the case that the synthesis has to be reported to others and the final format may therefore be contingent on the features of this wider forum. As was stated earlier in this book, the process of understanding failure, learning from that understanding and taking action is paramount and so the synthesis has to be developed and presented in a way that supports that process. The output may be a report to a client of some kind which may, in turn, be fed into the preparation of a training programme, the requirements and plans for the next phase of evolution, or into the drafting of a policy document. For a situation that has not experienced irretrievable failure the findings will probably suggest that remedy is possible, especially if the consequences of the failure were systemic but its causes were simple. On the other hand, in situations where the causes and the consequences were systemic, redesign may be necessary, in which case the findings can be fed into a process for generating an agenda for change. This idea of feeding the results into a design process is discussed in Chapter 9.

In an ideal world all the information about any failure situation would be available, but, in practice, understanding is like all knowledge; it is tentative, provisional and incomplete, and limited by lack of time and shortage of creative imagination. Failure is an emotive subject; it causes people to hide things, even trivialities, but in studying past failures one does at least have the benefit of hindsight. In the next chapter we shall be looking at two cases that provide ample opportunities to learn from IS failure.

References

Checkland, P.B. (1981) *Systems Thinking, Systems Practice*. John Wiley & Sons, Chichester.

Churchman, C.W. (1971) *The Design of Inquiring Systems*. Basic Books, New York.

Fortune, J. (1993) *Systems Paradigms*. Open University Press, Milton Keynes.

Jenkins, G.M. (1969) The systems approach. *Journal of Systems Engineering*, 1: 3–49.

Pearce, T. & Fortune, J. (2002) Taking account of human rights. In G. Ragsdell *et al.* (eds) *Systems Theory and Practice in the Knowledge Age*. Kluwer Academic/Plenum Publishers, New York, pp. 275–282.

Peters, G. & Fortune, J. (1992) Systemic methods for the analysis of failure. *Systems Practice*, 5: 529–542.

Chapter 8

INFORMATION
SYSTEMS IN PRACTICE

Introduction

When things go awry there are usually only a few people on the inside who know what happened; as little information as possible is made public and there is certainly no opportunity for outsiders to examine the history or to critique events. Sometimes, as in the cases described in Chapter 3, researchers have been following what happened and are able to publish accounts and analyses of such events. In the public sector, governmental bodies of various sorts also conduct inquiries and the reports they produce often enter the public domain. In the case of serious accidents there are bodies, such as the Health and Safety Executive in the UK, charged with investigating, making recommendations and, if necessary, undertaking prosecutions. If an accident is serious enough there will be an official inquiry. Similarly, when things go wrong in the administration of public affairs, several jurisdictions have what is called an official auditor or audit office that has responsibility for scrutinizing public spending and ensuring value for money. In England, The Comptroller and Auditor General, is an Officer of the House of Commons and is the head of the National Audit Office (NAO). Independent of government, The Comptroller and Auditor General certifies the accounts not only of all government departments but also of a wide range of other public sector bodies and has statutory authority to report to Parliament on the economy, efficiency and effectiveness with which government departments and other related bodies have used their resources.

With the permission of the NAO, this chapter draws extensively on two official reports of NAO inquiries into attempts to design, build and implement large-scale information systems. The first, the Benefits Payment Card project, was intended to replace the existing paper-based methods of paying social security benefits with a magnetic stripe payment card, and to automate the national network of post offices through which most benefits are paid across Great Britain and Northern Ireland. In May 1996, the Benefits Agency of the UK Department of Social Security and Post Office Counters Ltd jointly awarded a contract to Pathway, a subsidiary of the then ICL computer services group. The Benefits Payment Card project was cancelled in May 1999. At the time the contract was signed, it was planned to take 10 months to start a live trial of the full system intended to cover 24 different social benefits, such as disability allowances, and all of the 19 000 post offices then in the network. In fact, even this stage had not been reached at the time the contract was terminated nearly three years later.

The second report involved the Lord Chancellor's Department. In 1998 the Department signed a contract with ICL to develop a national standard Information Technology and Information System called Libra to support the work of magistrates' courts in England and Wales. Libra was to consist of both infrastructure and applications. The project hit problems and was renegotiated twice after contract signature. On the first occasion this was because ICL had overestimated the revenues and underestimated the costs of the contract and, on the second, because delays to the development, caused by a number of different factors, had increased ICL's costs. In July 2002, after considering the options available, the Department signed a variation to the contract with ICL to deliver only the national IT infrastructure and office automation facilities, and not the core software to support court operation or the system integration. In the period between 1998 and July 2002 costs more than doubled.

Neither of these cases is unique and they should not be read as critical reflections on government departments or particular suppliers. However, they do provide real examples of what can happen to IS projects in practice and thus provide valuable opportunities for learning.

The Benefits Payment Card project

In the UK, citizens who meet the appropriate criteria are entitled to a range of state-funded financial payments. These 'benefits' provide assistance for people on low incomes, for those who are disabled or seeking work and for others in a variety of other circumstances. From time to time the level of the benefits payable to an individual changes because the recipient's circumstances alter or the criteria for payment change or because overall levels of payment are revised. At the time this project was instigated many of the claimants receiving predictable and regular payments were issued in advance with books of dated coupons, called 'order books', that could be cashed at their local post offices. Others receiving different categories of payments were issued with 'girocheques' that could be cashed at post offices or paid into bank or building society accounts. The idea behind the Benefits Payment Card was to issue those entitled to these benefits with a single card that contained all the information necessary for their benefit payments to be authorized and for post offices to be automated so that changes to an individual's entitlement, as well as that person's identity, could be readily checked.

Three main parties were involved in the project: The Department of Social Security together with its Benefits Agency; Post Office Counters Ltd; and ICL plc, through a company called Pathway. Each of the parties is described more fully in Table 8.1.

The overall objectives of the Benefits Payment Card project were:

- To provide a virtually fraud-free method of paying benefits at post offices that was automated, had lower costs than the current paper-based processes, and administrative costs that reduced year on year.
- To extend automation to Post Office Counters Ltd's transactions for its other customers and other products and processes, thereby improving its competitiveness and efficiency.
- To enable full and speedy reconciliation of benefits payments, with accounting arrangements consistent with recognized accountancy practices.
- To provide an improved service to the customers of both Post Office Counters Ltd and the Department of Social Security.

The two commissioning parties, the Department of Social Security (DSS) and Post Office Counters Ltd, had a mutual interest in the success of the Benefits Payment Card, but their motives were different (see Table 8.2).

The objective of the DSS to reduce fraud was of particular significance to the project. Because many of the people who were entitled to benefits might not be able to visit the same (or in some cases any) post office each time a payment was due, there were various procedures that allowed payees to authorize others to claim on their behalf and for payment to be made at different post offices. For these and other reasons, fraud resulting from the misuse of order books and girocheques was estimated at over £100 million each year (see Table 8.3). The financial case for the Benefits Card Payment project was based on the DSS achieving the potential 'fraud savings' from the introduction of the new system. This meant that any significant delay in delivery would begin to erode the business case.

Table 8.1 The main players in the Benefits Payment Card project

	The Department of Social Security and the Department's Benefits Agency	Post Office Counters Ltd	ICL plc, through Pathway
Area of business	The Benefits Agency's purpose is to deliver benefits to the public through services that are active, customer focused, secure and accurate. They operate from a national network of several hundred local offices and from three central directorates. The Agency's Chief Executive is a member of the Management Board of the Department of Social Security and is accountable to ministers of that Department, and to Parliament as an Accounting Officer.	Operates a network of some 18 300 post offices, providing services such as postage, bill payment and financial services, to some 28 million customers each week. One of the three main businesses of the Post Office Counters Ltd, a public corporation established under the Post Office Act 1969. Through the Department of Trade and Industry, the government appoints the Post Office's management board.	Owned by Fujitsu of Japan, the company implements systems for major projects and provides services to a range of industries including retail, finance, telecommunications and the education, local and central government sectors. ICL plc participated in this project through a wholly-owned subsidiary, Pathway, that it formed for this specific purpose.
Financial and staffing	The Benefits Agency employs some 70 000 staff and pays over £80 billion each year through over 20 different social security benefits. Its operating costs were £2.4 billion in 1998/99. The other Agencies of the DSS are the Child Support Agency and the War Pensions Agency, which, with Departmental Headquarters and various statutory bodies, constitute a group with over 80 000 staff including the Benefits Agency.	In 1999–2000 Post Office Counters Ltd reported turnover of £1.17 billion and profits of £46 million before taxation and exceptional items. It directly employs 12 000 staff and has contracts with nearly 17 000 subpostmasters.	Operating in over 70 countries and employing over 20 000 people, ICL's revenues for the period ending March 1999 were £3.3 billion generating a pre-tax profit of £41 million before exceptional items.

Note: This table describes the situation at the time of the project. Since July 1999 all the organizations have undergone substantial change.
Source: National Audit Office (2000).

Table 8.2 Overall objectives of the Benefits Card Payment project

Objective	Department of Social Security	Post Office Counters Ltd
To provide a virtually fraud-free method of paying benefits at post offices that is automated, has lower end-to-end costs than the current paper-based process, with continuously reducing overall administration costs year on year.	X	
To automate Post Office Counters Ltd's other client transactions, its products and its support processes to improve competitiveness, increase efficiency, and to enable greater commercial opportunities for the business.		X
To enable full and speedy reconciliation of benefits payments, with accounting arrangements consistent with recognized accountancy practices.	X	
To provide an improved service to the parties' customers.	X	X

Source: National Audit Office (2000).

The project was vast in its investment, scale and complexity (see Table 8.4). It was also one of the first Information Systems and Technology contracts awarded under the Private Finance Initiative (PFI). The essence of the PFI is that the private sector supplier receives a contract to design, build, finance and operate an asset, and is paid for the provision of the service only as it is delivered to the public sector purchaser. In the context of Information Systems and Technology, government departments pay for the availability or use of the system to the standards laid down in the contract. In this way, many risks that would normally be borne by the public sector, such as higher than expected development or running costs, should, in theory at least, be carried by the private sector supplier.

Table 8.3 Comparison of the methods of benefit payment used by the Department of Social Security in terms of cost, volume and level of fraud

Method of benefit payment	Average direct cost (pence per transaction)	Share of benefits payments in 1998/99 (£ billion)	Share of benefits payments in 1998/99 (%)	Estimated fraud in 1998 (£ million)	Fraud rate[4] (%)
Order Book	49	51	63	85	1.7
Girocheques and payable orders	79	6	8	22	3.7
Bank Transfers[1,2]	1	24	29	None identified	
Payment Cards[3]	67	0.03	0	None identified	
Total		81	100	107	

Notes:
[1] The proportion of new claimants choosing payment by bank transfer ranges from 10% for Income Support recipients to 47% for retirement pensions and 54% for Child Benefit. Some 16 million customers use order books or girocheques and 8 million are paid by bank transfer. There is a continuing trend towards greater use of bank transfers, adding about half a million customers to the total each year. Transaction costs are rounded to the nearest penny.
[2] Transfers into claimants' bank accounts are cheaper to the DSS, in part because they transfer the cost of providing cash to the banking system already available to 85% of benefit recipients. This cost varies according to the method through which cash is dispensed, and the circumstances of the account owner. The cost of a bank transfer shown here is the direct cost to the DSS, and excludes any costs to banks, and costs of extending the Agency's systems.
[3] At the time it was cancelled, the payment card had been used to pay some £30 million of child benefit, to 37 000 customers in 205 out of over 18 000 post offices. The use of the card has since been stopped.
[4] Fraud figures are for misuse of instruments of payment only, and exclude other types of benefit fraud. The figures cited here reflect reductions in fraud achieved by an Electronic Stop Notice System in the Greater London area since the mid-1990s

Source: National Audit Office (2000).

Table 8.4 Key statistics of the Benefits Payment Card project

Estimated contract value (payments by DSS and Post Office):	£1 billion, net present value over 7 years
Number of post offices to be equipped:	Up to 20 000, with 40 000 counter points in Great Britain and Northern Ireland
Number of post office staff to be trained in use of the system:	67 000 staff, serving 28 million customers per week
Number of social security benefit recipients to be issued with Payment Cards:	17 million, claiming some 24 different benefits
Number and value of benefit transactions:	In 1999/2000 some 760 million payments worth £56 billion were made through post offices

Source: National Audit Office (2000).

Chronological history of the Benefits Payment Card project

Some of the key events in the life of the project are described in the next section. In the following sections the project and the way it was conducted are examined in more depth by looking at some of its special features.

'Initial go-live' trials

The DSS, Post Office Counters Ltd and Pathway were successful in rolling out a limited early version of the Benefits Payment Card hardware and software to 10 post offices in Stroud, Gloucestershire, by October 1996, close to their contractual timetable. As intended, this system had only partial functionality. For example:

- The system only supported the payment of child benefit, and only allowed a limited volume of transactions. Technically, the system was capable of processing other benefits, but it had yet to include additional security features that would assure the DSS that it could be entrusted with other higher risk benefits, and higher volumes.

- The system did not allow payees to collect benefit from a post office other than the one they had nominated.

Although the parties successfully implemented the limited 'initial go-live' as planned, the process of designing and developing a fully functional system proved much more complex and took much longer than had been expected. The overall timetable for completing the roll-out of the full system across the country slipped from 1999 to 2001 although development work continued, and further functionality was added through successive software releases, which were used in 205 post offices.

The replan and subsequent progress

During the second half of 1996, the DSS, Post Office Counters Ltd and Pathway became increasingly aware of the difficulties they faced in implementing the full Benefits Payment Card system. The DSS found that the complexity and resource requirements of their Customer Accounting and Payments System (CAPS) project, which was to feed data to Pathway's Card systems, had been greatly underestimated. At the same time they were aware, from their continuing liaison arrangements, that Pathway had encountered similar difficulties in its own work. Pathway also expressed concern about some aspects of the agreed high-level specification regarding security, which were central to the DSS's business case. Therefore, discussions were opened that led in February 1997 to a 'no-fault' replan involving all the parties of both projects. Under this agreement, all parties agreed to postpone the delivery dates by three months and to bear their own costs in doing so. The parties then committed to achieving the revised dates. The DSS agreed to continue development of Customer Accounting and Payment Systems (CAPS) separately from Pathway's development of software for the Card, while ensuring that the necessary technical interfaces were in place to meet Pathway's revised timetable. This was the first and only formal, contractual agreement to change delivery dates.

Despite the replan, the project continued to make slow progress. The replan envisaged, by 21 November 1997, a live trial to demonstrate sustained, satisfactory operation of child benefit payments and a range of post office functions in 300 post offices. Although Pathway delivered intermediate releases of software, the live trial was not completed.

Reconsideration of options

Following the failure to complete the live trial, the purchasers served a formal notice of breach of contract on Pathway. Pathway denied the claim and counter-asserted breach of obligations by the purchasers. In December 1997, Pathway wrote to the Benefits Agency suggesting three options:

1. Maintain the existing contract but with Pathway's prices raised by 30%.
2. Extend the contract by five years and raise prices by 5%.
3. Terminate the contract.

The DSS were not in a position to take unilateral action, but recognizing the continuing difficulties, sought interdepartmental discussions, involving primarily HM Treasury, the Department of Trade and Industry and the Prime Minister's office, to reach a wider cross-government solution. Post Office Counters Ltd and Pathway were also involved. An independent panel of experts was recruited to support an Inter-Departmental review of options that began in early 1998.

The objectives agreed by ministers collectively were:

- To aim to protect a nationwide network of post offices. This was defined as avoiding significant post office closures, though in the longer term it could mean changing the shape of the network to enable services to be accessed in different ways.
- To pay social security benefits in a way that is as cheap, as efficient, and as fraud free as possible (taking into account the costs of getting cash into claimants' hands) and consistent with welfare reform.
- To modernize the delivery of government services and information more generally, taking full advantage of new technology.
- To improve access to basic financial services, including banking services, for poorer members of the community and the socially excluded.
- To maintain a thriving IT sector in the UK, in which ICL is a key player, while ensuring that risks transferred through Private Finance projects do not end up with the taxpayer.
- To deliver best value overall for the taxpayer.

The three main options were (1) continuation or (2) cancellation of the entire project, involving both the automation of post offices and the introduction of the Benefits Payment Card, or (3) continuing with post office automation only. The independent panel of experts looked at financial and non-financial aspects and concluded that the project could deliver the functions required, but was unlikely to operate nationwide much before the end of 2001 – three years later than originally planned. They stressed that successful delivery would require renewed commitment from the parties and was not without risk. The cost of continuing was uncertain.

As stated earlier, the DSS's business case for the project was based on achieving the potential fraud savings from introducing the new system. This meant that any significant delay in delivery would begin to erode the business case (see Table 8.5).

Table 8.5 The erosion of the Department of Social Security's original business case, for the contract period 1996 to 2005

	Case as at project signature, April 1996 (£ million[2])	Case after project replan, May 1997 (£ million[3])	Case at cancellation, May 1999 (£ million[4])
Payment service costs	1477	1464	1112
Less: Administrative savings	1180	1022	598
Less: Fraud savings	1428	1395	765
Net saving[5]	1127	953	251
Net saving (discounted)[1]	667	564	148

Notes:
[1] Costs and savings are expressed as net present values discounted at 6% per annum compounded over the planned life of the project, and converted to constant May 1996 price levels. For comparability, all figures take the assumption that the contract ends in 2005.
[2] The 1996 Business Case compared the costs and benefits of the Card project against those of continuing with the existing paper-based payment arrangements. At that time a comprehensive move to payment through transfers to claimants' bank accounts was not an option under policy, though it remained the most cost-effective method of payment to the DSS.
[3] In early 1997 the comprehensive introduction of payment through bank transfers was still not an option under government policy, though it remained the DSS's preferred long-term option.
[4] By this stage, incoming Ministers had reopened the option of a comprehensive move to benefit payment through bank transfers, should the Card project fail. Also, Pathway had requested a contract extension or price increases.
[5] Running cost savings included planned reductions in the DSS's payments to Post Office Counters Ltd due to the introduction of the more efficient card system at post offices; and savings from replacing the operation of order books.
Source: Department of Social Security, quoted in National Audit Office (2000).

In May 1999 the government decided that removing the payment card from the project offered better value for money than complete cancellation. Furthermore, they reasoned that such a move would better protect the early automation of the Post Office, and was preferable to continuation. They devised a new strategy with the following key features:

- The Benefits Payment Card element of the project would be dropped, simplifying and assuring the automation of Post Office Counters Ltd.
- Automation of Post Office Counters Ltd would proceed, for completion by 2001.
- Benefits payments would be made by automated transfers to claimants' bank accounts; starting in 2003 and completing by 2005 – until 2003 existing arrangements would continue.
- People who wished to continue to collect their cash at post offices would continue to be able to do so. Post Office Counters Ltd would introduce suitable banking technology and commercial arrangements with banks to allow this to happen.
- Special arrangements would be made for the relatively few people for whom a bank account may remain an unsuitable option.

Features of the Benefits Payment Card Project

There are several features of the Benefits Card project that help to explain what happened and are drawn out within the NAO report. The full report devotes considerable attention to the assessment and management of risk and the implications of this project for other PFI projects. In doing so, it also highlights other features that warrant further description. Some are detailed below.

Management of Risks

The NAO concluded that the purchasers' joint procurement team made strenuous efforts to identify the risks of the project. In March 1995, seven months into the procurement stage, they compiled a comprehensive register comprising 224 risks. These covered the specific risks within the project and the wider business risks that could affect it. The register included virtually all those that could have been reasonably foreseen, such as:

- inadequately specified requirements;
- delays in the DSS's CAPS project which would link to the Card system;
- deterioration in services to customers, such as unacceptable queuing time at post offices; and
- poor performance by the supplier.

However, the NAO concluded that this register did not include assessments of probability and impact, nor did it allocate risks to 'owners' for management, or propose options to mitigate the risks. The NAO also found no evidence that it was then further developed into a fully-featured risk register and actively used in the project.

Specification of requirements

At the time the purchasers invited private sector interest their requirements were defined only at high level. A formal Statement of Service Requirements was only agreed by the DSS and Post Office Counters Ltd in February 1995 and issued to bidders in April 1995, eight months into the procurement. This statement changed subsequently. Consultants producing an assessment of 'lessons learned' for the purchasers in November 1997 reported that requirements had increased by between 10 and 20% in the period from April 1995 to February 1996. They said that the increases resulted from clarifications, new requirements not included in the original statement, and detailed documentation of the rules and constraints under which services were to be provided.

In October 1995, in an effort to draw together the detailed requirements, the purchasers started to set up a Requirements Catalogue. It was intended that the catalogue would provide detailed service definitions and that service providers would respond with solutions to them in their bids. However, in November 1995, in response to increasing concerns from the service providers and the purchasers about the time and cost of the procurement, the joint procurement authority that was established by the purchasers to manage the procurement stopped work on developing these service definitions. With the agreement of all three shortlisted bidders, the purchasers stated that detailed requirement definitions would be agreed with the selected supplier after the contract had been awarded, and invited tenders on the basis of higher level specifications. Though work on the Requirements Catalogue was stopped, the purchasers continued to direct additional information on their requirements to the bidders right up to the issue of the formal invitation to submit priced bids. Some 333 additional details and clarifications to requirements were issued between November 1995 and the end of January 1996.

'Agreements to agree'

The NAO reported, from their examination of the records, that when the contract was signed there were 289 'agreements to agree' the detail of the service contained in it, of which 38 remained to be agreed by Pathway with the DSS, 124 with Post Office Counters Ltd, and 127 with both clients jointly. Pathway told the NAO that they had expected these to be cleared within the first three months during a process of dropdown, but dropdown instead focused on legal arrangements rather than the technical and service aspects in the 'agreements to agree'. The DSS told the NAO that it had never been intended to resolve the 'agreements to agree' during dropdown, only the mechanisms for completing them. Some of the outstanding agreements were relatively minor, such as the design of the logos to appear on the card, whereas others were more significant. The NAO concluded that resolving the more important 'agreements to agree' was essential in order to be able to finalize the detailed design of the system and deliver the full service.

Project Management arrangements

When the contract was awarded to Pathway in May 1996, the DSS and Post Office Counters Ltd established a joint Delivery Authority to manage the development, system acceptance and roll-out phases. The Authority was staffed and funded jointly by DSS and Post Office Counters Ltd. This body effectively stood between Pathway and the intended users of the system in the Department of Social Security and Post Office Counters Ltd. The Project Steering Committee included the Chief Executive of ICL and Managing Director of Pathway, as well as the Chief Executive of the Benefits Agency and the Managing Director of Post Office Counters Ltd. Similarly, below the Steering Committee the Board included the Managing Director and Programme Director of Pathway. Progress against the project plan was regularly reported to the Steering Committee and Board. Figure 8.1 depicts the relationships between the various bodies.

The Delivery Authority established a new risk register incorporating risks identified earlier. Most risks were managed within the Delivery Authority and were described in regular highlighted reports made to the new Project Director and his team. Key risks and issues were reported to the Board and the Steering Committee. The NAO examination of the Delivery Authority's risk register revealed that not all ongoing risks were captured from the procurement phase. For the majority of identified risks the register did not show the countermeasures or mitigating action taken. The NAO

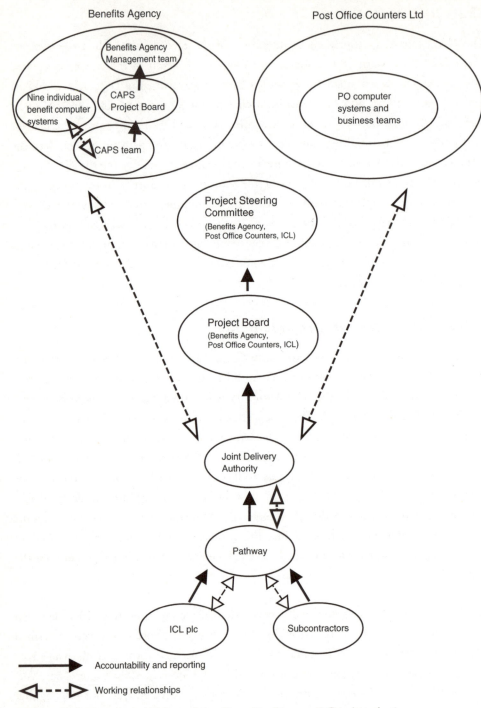

Figure 8.1   The organization of the Benefits Payment Card project
(*Source*: National Audit Office, 2000)

also noted that assessments of the probability of risks occurring were not applied consistently since there were inconsistencies in the numerical systems used.

None of the project documentation the NAO saw provided evidence of the use of project planning tools to identify the potential impact of delay. The NAO reported:

> Project plans maintained by Pathway and by the Delivery Authority appeared to lack 'earliest' and 'latest' estimates of duration for each major activity, using instead only single point estimates. We found no evidence of the use of sensitivity analysis in detailed project plans; this resulted in repeated instances of 'unforeseen' project slippage. Such estimates are a fundamental cornerstone to all project planning, and delivery measurement.

> (National Audit Office, 2000, p. 71)

Emerging complexity of the benefit arrangements

Customer Surveys in late 1995 had emphasized the need to continue to provide flexibility for payees in terms of the way they could collect their benefits – for example, the freedom to be able to use a post office other than their 'normal' one and to nominate other people (agents) to collect benefit on their behalf either on a temporary or a regular basis. Increased emphasis on the importance of service delivery to benefit customers evidently emphasized the need to replicate existing payment rules, as opposed to re-engineering a simpler process.

Pathway told the NAO that the emergence of complexity in the service requirement after the contract was signed caused them acute problems in two main areas:

- *Temporary tokens*   The arrangements that apply when someone collects a benefit (prior to issue of a Card) or does so on behalf of another person at short notice on a temporary basis.
- *Extended verification processes*   The process through which the DSS could change the targeting of identity checks on particular groups of payees. Payees were to be asked to verify their identity at the counter by giving personal details in answer to computer-generated questions when presenting their payment card.

Pathway told the NAO that complexity lay not so much in each individual area but in the way they combined across the different types of benefit recipient (normal beneficiaries, permanent agents, temporary agents, and alternative payees). Different rules for different benefits needed to be reconciled. Complexity thus related to a small minority of payment collections (estimated to be between 1 and 5%), often where agents collected more than one benefit. Pathway told the NAO that the DSS appeared inflexible in simplifying the application of rules to lessen the complexity of the resulting system. The NAO noted that the DSS had attempted simplification, but were constrained by legislation and by the need to meet benefit recipients' expectations in this difficult area.

The DSS gave the NAO their own perspective of how complexity emerged in areas identified by Pathway. On the issue of verification procedures, the DSS felt that they had sought to preserve their requirement for flexibility to target verification procedures in response to changing patterns of fraud. They had agreed to Pathway developing initial software using 'hard coding', but had required the full version to be written using 'soft-coding', to ensure that verification questions could be targeted effectively in practice.

Pathway also noted that at the time the contract was signed there was no authoritative document which collated and reconciled all the different rules that governed payment of different benefits. The rules differed between benefits, partly for historical reasons, and partly because the differing circumstances of various types of claimants determined the extent of their reliance on emergency payments and on agents to collect benefit on their behalf. This proved to be a very difficult area to resolve. It required the DSS and Pathway to trace back the payment practices of different benefits to their, often conflicting, regulations and legislation and then to produce a single set of rules that could be programmed into the Card system. Pathway produced the first version of the new document which documented these rules in 1996 and submitted it to the DSS for agreement. Five subsequent iterations followed, during which time the DSS examined at length the need to embark on the difficult parliamentary processes of changing legislation. The document was not finally agreed until February 1999. Ironically, the agreement came just before the Card project was cancelled. Pathway designed and redesigned software while these iterations continued. Pathway's interpretation of these events was not completely shared by the DSS who told the NAO that they had provided a statement of rules they had considered definitive as early as October 1996, and had worked hard with Pathway on the correct interpretation of these rules.

Pathway's expectations

The project initially proceeded on the basis of proposals from Pathway that it would involve mainly the integration of existing software packages. In the event, the greater than expected complexity of the service requirement obliged Pathway to undertake much more development of new software than it had planned for in its winning bid. This had major implications for the degree of difficulty of the project.

Pathway told the NAO that it had expected more scope to redesign the DSS's business rules and requirements so that software could be based more closely on the solution installed in the initial 10 post offices in September 1996. The 'initial go-live' was always intended to be an interim system. It did not offer full functionality, and included some extemporized processes that would have to be replaced with permanent software for the subsequent roll-out to 200 post offices. It was a development based on software that was running live in post offices in Ireland. The purchasers had, during the procurement phase of the project, identified as an issue the extent to which Pathway would have to change software running on the system in Ireland.

Interconnectedness of the CAPS project and the Benefits Payment Card project

At the time the Benefits Payment Card contract was signed, the proposed CAPS timetable specified that, by December 1996, 50% of all post offices would have been converted and half of all CAPS benefit payments would be transacted using the new Benefits Payment Card. Both systems would continue to roll out in parallel over the following two years. The CAPS development project was managed by the DSS and was comparable in size and complexity to the Benefits Payment Card development. All three of the bidders shortlisted for the Benefits Payment Card project told the NAO that they were conscious of the size and complexity of CAPS and that any slippage in its development would be likely to affect the Benefits Payment Card project.

The NAO view was that the risks of late delivery of CAPS were not well managed prior to the replan of the whole CAPS and Benefits Payment Card programme in February 1997. A new project director took up post in mid-1996, around the time that the Benefits Payment Card contract was awarded to Pathway. He found that the project had not been appropriately resourced. The DSS also commissioned a review by consultants Ernst & Young. In December 1996 they reported:

- a lack of project management expertise at the right level within the CAPS senior management team;
- a focus on short-term objectives to support the initial go-live, at the expense of developing a set of plans and designs for the programme as a whole; and
- doubts over the strength of financial projections and cost control.

Ernst & Young made recommendations for improved management and planning which the DSS implemented to reduce the risk of subsequent slippage on CAPS. Although CAPS had contributed to delays in the project up to the replan in February 1997, the DSS thereafter successfully released software and data from CAPS in time for the equivalent releases of Payment Card software by Pathway. NAO found no evidence that, from then onwards, the releases of CAPS software had delayed the implementation of the Benefits Payment Card.

Implications of cancellation of the Benefits Payment Card project for the various parties

The cancellation of the project had implications for benefit claimants who would not be able to gain from the service improvements and other advantages stated for the payment card, such as quicker response to changes in their entitlement. ICL wrote off project development costs of £180 million in June 1999, while the project received much negative publicity in the national, business and specialist press at the time.

DSS's positive business case for the project reduced from £667 million net present value to £148 million, due mainly to the delay in achieving estimated fraud savings. The DSS also lost its planned savings in the cost of administering order books, but these were broadly matched by savings in lower than expected payments to Pathway for processing card transactions. Some £127 million of the £270 million costs of their CAPS program was attributed to features required to link to the Benefits Payment Card. However, by subsequently introducing an electronic system for the control of order books, the DSS still hoped to eliminate 85% of fraudulent misuse of order books. By moving over to payment by bank transfer between 2003 and 2005, the DSS also sought to make administrative savings earlier than if the Payment Card project had continued.

With the abandonment of the Benefits Payment Card project, Post Office Counters Ltd had to manage the project to automate its offices on its own. Under standard accounting practice, the Post Office cannot take account of income that may be generated in the future but cannot be guaranteed. Therefore, in November 1999, Post Office Counters Ltd was obliged to record in its accounts an exceptional charge of £571 million 'for acquiring an asset which does not at this stage yield sufficient income to justify the cost'. Of greater potential significance, the decision to move to bank transfer as a method of paying benefits left Post Office Counters Ltd and its sub-postmasters exposed to the risks of loss of benefit payment business and the associated indirect advantage of payees' other business.

Conclusion

There were many features of this project that increased the likelihood that it would not be completely successful. The complexity of the task was not fully appreciated originally, and the attempts to combine the different interests of the two purchasers and the supplier could have proved to be problematic. The NAO view was that

> the project had a high probability of failure as soon as the contract was signed, though this was not fully evident at the time. The pressures this caused during the implementation stage would have severely tested any project organization.

Project Libra

Magistrates' courts are the lowest level of court in England and Wales. Approximately 95% of criminal cases are dealt with at this level and do not proceed to higher courts. At the time of the Libra project, their administration was the responsibility of local administrative bodies called Magistrates' Courts Committees that employed more than 10 000 staff. Although they were independent bodies, the Magistrates' Courts Committees were answerable for their performance to the Lord Chancellor, but each Committee decided on how best to provide an efficient and effective service within its area. Following from the Police and Magistrates' Courts Act 1994, the number of Committees was being reduced from 105 to 42. Further changes were later included in the Courts Reform Bill introduced in 2002, paving the way for a merger of the magistrates' courts with the other criminal, civil and family courts in England and Wales.

The call for improvement in the information systems and information technology to support magistrates has a long history. In 1981 the Public Accounts Committee criticized the Home Office for its lack of initiative in examining the scope for computerization of magistrates' courts and not encouraging appropriate computerization.

The Committee recommended that the Home Office should look at opportunities for improving efficiency and economy through further computerization and coordination, and that it should monitor the performance of existing systems. In 1989 an internal Home Office scrutiny of magistrates' courts (the 'Le Vay' report) recommended that a common IT strategy for magistrates' courts should be developed as quickly as possible.

There followed a series of attempts to improve the information systems that support magistrates' courts, and to allow information to be shared with other courts and agencies such as the police, prisons, the probation service and the Crown Prosecution Service. In January 1992, the Home Office appointed the consultants Price Waterhouse to develop a national IT system. In August 1992, after responsibility for the magistrates' courts service had passed to the Lord Chancellor's Department, the contract with Price Waterhouse was terminated 'on the grounds that the firm's work was substandard and it had not delivered as expected under the contract. The Department initiated action for breach of contract', and 'in May 1995, the Department accepted PriceWaterhouse's offer of £1.375 million in full settlement'.

In 1994 the Department let contracts to a set of providers of training, software and hardware – Admiral (development of the system and training), FI (software support), and ICL, Digital and Bull (hardware) – for the development of a national Magistrates' Courts Standard System (MASS). By September 1996, the basic MASS software had been written, but not tested. At that time, after an independent review showed that the Department's strategy for delivery of the project was flawed, the Department terminated all existing contracts. The Department paid its MASS contractors some £6.8 million. The NAO report the principal reasons for cancellation as: the lack of experienced and strong project management; the problems inherent in managing a disparate set of suppliers; and the extending timescales.

In October 1996, the Department started to procure a PFI contract for Libra. Libra was the name given to the project to deliver national standard information systems services to improve the efficiency and effectiveness of the administration and management of magistrates' courts in England and Wales. The Department received 19 expressions of interest in response to the notice in the *Official Journal of the European Communities*, but only three responded to the Business Prospectus. These were (i) ICL and Unisys, with ICL eventually taking the prime contractor role; (ii) EDS, with STL Technologies as subcontractor; and (iii) TRW/Bull. TRW/Bull dropped out after being shortlisted as it felt it did not have sufficient resources in the UK to undertake the project. Although

Table 8.6 The objectives of the Libra project

1. To achieve common standards of practice in relation to: the general management of magistrates' courts and their administration; case data; case management; accounting and enforcement procedures; management information and financial controls; and to ensure the effective and efficient operation of magistrates' courts.
2. To enable courts to process cases as rapidly and efficiently as possible with due regard to the overriding considerations of quality of justice, the statutory obligations of courts and good practice.
3. To enable Magistrates' Courts Committees to reduce, as far as practicable, delays to members of the public and to representatives of other organizations.
4. To enable courts to meet their statutory obligations for accurate record-keeping in as efficient a manner as possible.
5. To enable courts to manage their statutory accounting functions more efficiently and effectively.
6. To standardize the facilities and increase the scope for electronic interchange of data between the magistrates' courts and other organizations, to avoid unnecessary repetition of data input procedures and reduce delays.
7. To provide functionality which exceeds that of present systems and includes the additional requirements stated in the statement of business requirement, without a reduction in efficiency.
8. To provide a basis for more flexible contingency planning.
9. To provide greater resilience in systems with an improved capability to deal with disaster recovery.
10. To provide economies of scale in training requirements and to increase the potential for mobility and interchange of staff by reducing the need for retraining at new sites.
11. To promote the smooth introduction of new functions and procedures resulting from changes in legislation, case law or policy.
12. To provide a migration path by automatic transfer of data from existing computer systems.
13. To provide for automated management and official statistical information.
14. To provide a standard terminology/glossary of terms in order to help to support common practice.

Source: Lord Chancellor's Department. Statement of Business Requirements, 1997; quoted in National Audit Office (2003).

EDS submitted a detailed proposal, by May 1998 ICL was the only company to respond to the final invitation to tender. In December 1998, the Department awarded ICL a contract for £184 million over 10.5 years.

In broad terms, the Libra project involved a national IT infrastructure of standard office software and hardware, a set of applications to support court work such as case management, and accounting, and electronic links with the other criminal justice agencies such as police, Crown Prosecution Service, probation service, prisons, the Crown Court and the Driver and Vehicle Licensing Agency.

The detailed objectives of the Libra project are given in Table 8.6.

Chronological history of the Libra project

As with the account of the Benefits Payment Card project, some of the key events in the life of the project are described below, and in the following sections, aspects of the project and the way it was conducted are examined in more depth.

The Libra project got off to a slow start. The procurement of Libra took over two years instead of the 14 months originally envisaged. The Department initiated the procurement in October 1996 but the contract was not signed until December 1998. The NAO concluded that the three main reasons for the procurement timetable being longer than expected were:

1. the time needed to get full involvement and agreement of users to the Statement of Business Requirement from the then 96 Magistrates' Courts Committees;
2. the time taken to get complete and satisfactory descriptions of each bidders' solution and plans; and
3. the winning bidder delaying contract signature through revising its bid.

ICL had originally proposed a cost of £146 million but this increased to £184 million by the time the contract was signed. £11 million of the increase was to allow for earlier delivery of the infrastructure and bespoke software, and £15 million was for incentive payments. ICL originally proposed a start date of January 1999 and a three-year development timescale, with the infrastructure and bespoke software being delivered at the same time. Libra's first local trial was due in December 2001. During post-tender negotiations, ICL offered to reduce the development timescale from three years to two. The Department declined that offer but agreed that ICL's plans showed that a 2.5-year timescale was achievable. The target for the first trial was brought forward to July 2001, with roll-out to be completed by March 2004. In addition, the contract would run for eight years from acceptance at the first Magistrates' Courts Committee and would end in July 2009, giving a total contract length of 10.5 years, of which five years would be full operation. The contract could also be extended twice by two years each time, giving a possible maximum contract length of 14.5 years.

In October 1999, some 10 months after contract signature, ICL formally asked to renegotiate the Libra contract on the grounds that their cash flow forecasts showed a £39 million deficit over the life of the deal. ICL said that it would be unable to continue with Libra if this gap could not be closed. At £10 million, the potential cost to ICL of walking away was lower than the loss it was forecasting.

The Department employed consultants Ernst & Young to assess ICL's capability of delivering the contract. Ernst & Young concluded that the position was worse than ICL had declared: ICL's financial model contained major flaws, was too complex and could not be relied upon as a basis for making business decisions. The Department and ICL agreed that, to establish a proper baseline for negotiations, a new financial model should be produced and jointly paid for and owned by the two parties. The new financial model corrected some of the flawed assumptions in the original model and, as a consequence, showed a cumulative deficit for ICL of £47 million over the life of the deal. PACE, a firm of independent consultants employed by the Department, considered that the project should be saved on the grounds that it was basically sound; that the potential benefits confirmed the strategic importance of Libra to the criminal justice system as a whole; and that the project was too important to allow ICL to default. Therefore, in May 2000 the Department and ICL signed a revised contract for the delivery of Libra. The value of the contract increased from £184 million to £319 million. The increase in costs was mainly for an extra four years of service at the end of the contract and for an earlier roll-out of the infrastructure. The Department and ICL agreed that the infrastructure and office automation service would be delivered nine months ahead of the scheduled implementation of the core application at each site. The Department gained two benefits from the earlier roll-out of the infrastructure. First, the core application, once developed and accepted, could be rolled out more quickly nationally as the infrastructure would already be in place. Secondly, Magistrates' Courts Committees would benefit sooner from support for basic office functions (for example, e-mail) with other courts and agencies within the criminal justice system. The advantage to ICL was that it would receive income under the deal at an earlier date.

A number of other changes were made to the contract. For example, the Department would pay £5 million on delivery of the final version of the functional specification following acceptance of the core application at the first site in Suffolk in July 2001, and £10 million on acceptance of the core application at Suffolk in return for the title to the intellectual property rights. The new contract gave the Department access to ICL's financial model and introduced sharing of excess profits.

In October 2000, ICL informed the Department that it would not be able to deliver all the software to the first site in Suffolk by the target date of July 2001. A joint review of ICL's plans recommended that criminal cases software should be delivered in July 2001, followed by the remainder 10 weeks later.

In February 2001, ICL appointed a new senior management team that insisted on changing the direction of the project by agreeing a new method for documenting the Libra requirements definition. The new approach required a definitive document against which the product could be developed and formally tested, and would address a number of integration problems. In June 2001, the new team was able to indicate formally that ICL would not be able to implement the core software due in Suffolk until May 2003.

ICL also informed the Department that it was in financial difficulties with the contract even at the price renegotiated a year before. In September 2001, ICL produced a new financial model, which indicated a maximum potential loss on the project, if it continued to 2013, of £200 million. ICL said that its parent company, Fujitsu, would repudiate the contract unless the Department negotiated to cover the loss. As in the case of the first renegotiation, the maximum liability for ICL walking away was lower than the loss it was forecasting.

As part of a wider reorganization, on 1 August 2001 senior client management of the Libra project moved to a new team in the Department's Court Service Agency. This team reviewed the alternatives of acceding to the proposed repudiation of the contract or entering into renegotiation. ICL had set deadlines of 30 September for a legally binding commitment to renegotiate and 31 January 2002 to complete the deal. Having reviewed the history of the situation and in recognition of a number of factors, including there being no developed contingency plan and users being impressed with some of the on-screen developments, a legally binding memorandum of understanding was signed on 5 October 2001 which ran initially until 31 January (later extended to 8 March 2002).

On 8 February 2002, ICL quoted a new price of £400 million for the enhanced infrastructure and full core application. The Department considered that this price was not affordable and did not provide value for money. On 26 February 2002, after further negotiations, ICL reduced its price to £384 million, although it was not a finalized price. ICL later offered an alternative solution with a different technical architecture, delivery plan and further reduced scope. But the Department considered the plan to be flawed. The reduction in scope was not considered acceptable and the projected timescales unachievable. It therefore decided not to proceed any longer with one contractor for the Libra project but to undertake fresh negotiations with a view to a disaggregated approach, securing infrastructure, application and integration services from separate suppliers. A £232 million contract for ICL to continue to provide and service the infrastructure element of Libra was signed on 23 July 2002. Table 8.7 summarizes the time-line for the project.

Features of the Libra project

Relationship between magistrates' courts and the Lord Chancellor's Department

Although, at the time of the project, the Lord Chancellor was accountable to Parliament for the operation of the magistrates' courts, they were locally administered. Magistrates' Courts Committees were independent bodies responsible for the effective administration of the magistrates' courts in their area. The Department's role was to issue guidance and encourage Magistrates' Courts Committees to adopt the project. Since 1999, the Lord Chancellor had reserve powers to require them to take specified goods and services if, in his opinion, it was in the interests of the service as a whole. However, these powers were not exercised. The Department did not have the power to dictate how Magistrates' Courts Committees should use the services provided. The administration and responsibilities of magistrates' courts have been through a number of changes before and since this project. Table 8.8 summarizes the main changes at that time.

Because of their independence, the Magistrates' Courts Committees showed considerable differences in the procedures and forms used to implement legislation and central

Table 8.7 The chronology of the Libra project

Date	Event
Oct. 96	The Department started to procure a PFI contract.
Nov. 96	The Department received 19 expressions of interest in response to a notice in the *Official Journal of the European Communities*.
Sep. 97	Two bidders (ICL and EDS) submitted detailed proposals.
May 98	EDS declined to submit a response to the Invitation to Tender.
May 98	ICL submitted the only bid for £146 million.
Jul. 98	ICL was chosen as the preferred bidder.
Oct. 98	ICL increased its bid from £146 million to £184 million.
Dec. 98	The Department awarded the contract to ICL after assessing ICL's offer as affordable and value for money. The contract was for £184 million over 10.5 years.
Oct. 99	ICL sought a renegotiation of the contract as its cash flow forecasts showed a £39 million deficit over the life of the deal.
May 00	The Department and ICL signed a revised contract for £319 million over 14.5 years. The increased cost was mainly for an extra four years of service and for earlier roll-out of the infrastructure.
Nov. 00	ICL informed the Department that it would only be able to deliver criminal cases software to the first site in Suffolk by the target date of July 2001, with software for family and licensing cases to be delivered 10 weeks later.
Feb.–Jun. 2001	ICL brought in a new management team who re-evaluated the plan and assessed that it was not deliverable.
Jun. 01	ICL told the Department that its forecast losses were now so high that it could not continue with the contract unless it was substantially renegotiated.

Table 8.7 *(Continued)*

Date	Event
Jul. 01	The Court Service, an Executive Agency of the Department, took over responsibility for the project. ICL was in breach of the contract for failing to meet the delivery date for core software at the first site. The Department decided to negotiate with ICL rather than terminate the contract and sue for damages. The Department started to consider other options for continuing with Libra.
Sep. 01	ICL told the Department that its maximum potential loss on the project was £200 million and that it would repudiate the contract unless the Department negotiated to cover the loss.
Oct. 01	The Department and ICL signed a legally binding Memorandum of Understanding, which placed the Department in a less favourable position than simply continuing with the existing contractual arrangements and relying on its contractual rights.
Feb. 02	On grounds of value for money and affordability the Department could not reach agreement with ICL for ICL to continue with the whole contract.
Jul. 02	The Department signed a revised contract with ICL (by then known as Fujitsu Services) for £232 million over 8.5 years to supply only the infrastructure element of Libra.

Source: Lord Chancellor's Department, quoted in National Audit Office (2003).

government policy. One example is the use of their own format for case file sheets and legal aid applications.

Project scope

In part, because the Department did not have the authority to impose business process change on the independent Magistrates' Courts Committees and because they had been

Table 8.8 The main changes affecting magistrates' courts since 1994

1994	The Police and Magistrates' Courts Act reformed the organization and management of the Magistrates' Courts Committees, providing clearer lines of accountability, both locally and with central government, and allowed the amalgamation of Committees.
1994–1997	A number of voluntary amalgamations took place, reducing the number of Magistrates' Courts Committees from 105 to 96.
1999–2001	A major programme of amalgamations took place reducing the number of Committees from 96 to 42, aligned with police authority boundaries.
April 2001	Magistrates' courts took over responsibility for enforcement of fines from the police.
October 2001	Lord Justice Auld's report 'Review of the Criminal Courts in England and Wales' published, recommending major changes to the criminal courts.
2002–2003	Courts Reform Bill introduced, paving the way for the unification of the criminal courts. This is expected to result in a single agency covering all courts in England and Wales by April 2005.

Source: Lord Chancellor's Department quoted in National Audit Office (2003)

through several recent changes, the Department's objectives for Libra were to maintain and improve service and not to attempt further major change. So the Department did not seek to redesign business processes in parallel with the development of a new IT system.

Specification of requirements

There are a number of ways in which the requirements were clarified or changed in the course of the project. When, in February 2001, ICL appointed a new senior management team they insisted on agreeing a new method for documenting the Libra requirements definition. It concluded that the Statement of Business Requirement was insufficiently detailed to enable it to be sure of the Department's requirements. In the spring of 2001, ICL initiated a process to document the overall business environment within which Libra would operate. This involved the Department, Magistrates' Courts

Committees and ICL in a series of workshops with the intention of preparing the logical requirements definition. The NAO stated that this 'effectively rendered nugatory over a year's worth of Magistrates' Courts Committee and Departmental staff effort in providing information to and reviewing documents from ICL in its original approach to requirements definition.'

Even in terms of hardware there were substantial changes. ICL had based its initial costs on assumptions that it would provide 5000 new workstations and take over up to 3500 existing workstations in the Magistrates' Courts Committees. During the renegotiations in 2000, the Department agreed to new standard workstations for all users, and the number of workstations was recalculated, resulting in a revised requirement for 8000 workstations plus 1500 for in-court computing. The Department later had to revise that estimate further when it became aware that the information supplied by Magistrates' Courts Committees was for full-time equivalents. A headcount figure, together with a further increase as a consequence of the transfer of enforcement from the police to the courts, resulted in a requirement for 11 000 workstations as part of the Memorandum of Understanding negotiations in 2001.

ICL's expectations

During the original procurement of the PFI deal, bidders were provided with the MASS software that had already been developed for the Department, together with associated documentation. ICL based its bid on developing the MASS software, which included an initial three-month evaluation of the software, and a positive outcome from that evaluation. Within three months of signing the contract ICL had evaluated the MASS software and chosen to proceed with its own software development instead.

ICL's financial model

The NAO is concerned with examining the economy, efficiency and effectiveness of the public sector and therefore it does not provide much insight into how ICL ended up revising their business model on several occasions. The NAO were concerned with reviewing Public Finance Initiatives such as this, and they do spend some time in their report reviewing the decision to let the tender to ICL when, by the end of the procurement, they were effectively the only formal bidder. ICL was chosen as the preferred bidder although the Department was aware of the problems ICL was having with the Benefits Card Project. The NAO view is that these factors made it 'even more important for the Department to satisfy itself thoroughly as to the technical competence of the bidder to deliver a project of such size and complexity. With hindsight, the Department should also have verified that the financial model on which the tender was based was sound and reflected the Department's requirements, although at the time Treasury Task Force advice was that this was not a requirement.' As stated earlier, once ICL realized in 1999 that they had problems with their business model the Department and ICL jointly paid for a new model that they subsequently shared.

Aspects of project management

Once the contract was procured, the Departmental staff involved stayed to manage the contract. On the ICL side, the Business Director from the negotiating team remained on the contract until a new Business Director was appointed in May 1999, and at a similar time, the ICL Project Director, who had also been involved in the procurement phase, was replaced. In November 2000, the ICL Business Director responsible for the project retired and a permanent replacement arrived in February 2001. Further changes occurred early in the autumn of 2001 with the appointment of a new management team for the period of the contract renegotiation.

Because of the time pressures, ICL started writing detailed computer programs before it had developed a full functional specification. It had started with the 'waterfall' approach to system development (see systems development life cycle, Chapter 2) and developed a functional specification, which was found to be deficient for its purpose. It therefore switched to an iterative approach with developers working with users to develop the system in small components, steadily adding more and more functionality. This parallel 'joint application design' approach to system development resulted in significantly improved productivity, but integration problems were also encountered.

Conclusion

One of the internal reviews of the project, in mid-2001, identified major weaknesses in the development process. The NAO report that the Department perceived this problem as a failure by ICL to provide the quality of business analysis expected under the contract; and ICL perceived the problem as a consequence of the awkward relationship between the Department and Magistrates' Courts Committees, which resulted in the Department being unable to act as a traditional user/customer, and the Committees being too fragmented to carry out such a role effectively. The review team thought that both perceptions had validity.

The review team also found that the contract was widely (though not unanimously) regarded by the Department as unworkable, and the ICL team, at the time of the NAO report, said they regarded the contract as having been undeliverable. The contract had exposed, and continued to expose, ICL to considerable financial risk, without giving ICL sufficient control to manage that risk. At the time the July 2002 contract was signed, ICL had written off £32.5 million as a result of cancellation of the software development element of the contract.

References

National Audit Office (2000) *The Cancellation of the Benefits Payment Card Project.* The Stationery Office, London.

National Audit Office (2003) *New IT Systems for Magistrates' Courts: The Libra Project.* The Stationery Office, London.

Chapter 9

USING THE APPROACH TO LOOK FORWARD: ELECTRONIC PATIENT RECORDS

Introduction

A 1993 paper on electronic patient records had a very revealing title; it used a semantic nicety which many of us in the academic world have employed when our research hasn't taken us quite as far as we hoped it would. It was entitled 'Toward an electronic patient record'. And yet information technology was by then already well established in the health care field. In the USA and Canada alone, millions of dollars had been spent on electronic patient record systems. What had gone wrong? Why were electronic patient records not well established in acute hospitals? This chapter describes a study, carried out for the Department of Health, which sought to answer those questions.

The main purpose of the chapter is to illustrate the process of using the Systems Failures Approach, but in so doing it covers two topics of growing significance: the design and implementation of information systems and the systemic nature of modern health care management.

Medical records

The medical record lies at the very heart of health care and its management. Wrenn *et al.* (1993), for example, make its importance plain:

> It is the primary way health professionals communicate with one another, allows information to be preserved, and facilitates continuity of care. It is the source document when questions of medical negligence or malpractice arise. Under the new relative value resource based system reimbursement scheme [in

use in the US], documentation affects physician reimbursement. It often is the only information used in quality assurance activities. Finally, the record can serve as a source of data for clinical research as well as research into 'process of care' for purposes of planning strategies to impact on the overall cost of health care delivery locally and nationally.

(Wrenn *et al.*, 1993, p. 809)

Despite their importance there is strong evidence that many medical records are incomplete and/or inaccurate. For example, Patel, Mould and Webb (1993) report the findings of a study that looked at the extent to which hospital records conformed to the *Guidelines for Clinicians on Medical Records and Notes* produced by the Royal College of Surgeons (1990). Analysis of notes of 100 consecutive discharges from two surgical units at different hospitals showed that, overall, only about 66% of the entries specified by College *Guidelines* were both present and correct, with 'regular update of notes, post-operative instructions, comments about post-operative recovery, the record of advice given to relatives and incorrect consent' all identified as 'substandard categories'.

Even where individual records are well kept the formats and methods of storage used do not allow equivalent information from large numbers of records to be extracted easily, thus eroding the value of the information as a research resource.

The gains that would be derived from an electronic system have been recognized for some time. In 1988, for example, McDonald and Tierney (1988, p. 3433) identified three kinds of benefits:

(1) improved logistics and organization of the medical record to speed care and improve care givers' efficiency;
(2) automatic computer review of the medical record to limit errors and control costs;
(3) systematic analysis of past clinical experience to guide future practices and policies.

The EPR project

In the UK in the early 1990s several strands started to come together which convinced people that the time was right to have computer-based patient record systems. Recent changes in information technology meant that processing had become faster and cheaper, and user-friendly graphical interfaces could also be provided relatively inexpensively. A surge of interest in the USA, which resulted in a series of papers on the topic being presented at the American Medical Informatics Association, fired the interest of UK delegates from the Department of Health and the Medical Royal Colleges. They recognized that the integrated NHS organization and structure meant that it might be easier to carry out the development work that could lead to generic, integrated systems. This work would also be able to feed off a Clinical Terms Project which was already under way to produce a thesaurus of terms used in health care through which clinicians could communicate.

In the light of all these good omens, the Department of Health in the UK decided in the spring of 1993 to give the go-ahead to the 'electronic patient record (EPR) project', a large, three-year strategic research and development programme. It was launched under the management of a Programme Board made up of clinicians and representatives of the Department of Health, NHS management and suppliers at the beginning of 1994.

The mission statement adopted by the Programme Board was as follows:

> The Project will help doctors, nurses and other health care professionals [henceforth collectively referred to as clinicians] to give better care to patients through the use of Electronic Patient Record systems. It will show the potential benefits of EPR systems by working in acute hospitals with clinicians, managers, suppliers and the Department of Health to produce working demonstrations and by supporting a programme of research into the EPR and related problems.

The following objectives were set for the project:

1. To improve patient care through Electronic Patient Record systems and to explore the use of and value to clinicians of generic, integrated EPR systems in acute hospitals.
2. To build two demonstrator systems in acute hospitals using a prototyping approach to explore the issues relating to the EPR with a view to:
   (a) capturing the interest of the clinical professions;
   (b) convincing managers of the benefits of EPR systems;
   (c) influencing suppliers to develop the next generation of hospital information technology;
   (d) learning lessons of wider relevance to other person-based programmes.

3. To identify potential benefits of EPR, both tangible and intangible, to quantify their cost and to develop a methodology to ensure realization of cost-effective benefits.

4. To understand the cultural issues relating to the EPR within and between departments in acute hospitals, between acute hospitals, and between acute hospitals and the long-stay and community services, including general practice, at national level.

5. To examine the issues concerning communication in an EPR system within an acute hospital and between it and other related systems.

6. To investigate the technical issues involved in building and implementing EPR systems.

7. To undertake a programme of research and development work to underpin the development of the EPR demonstrators.

8. To ensure that the EPR Project makes maximum use of the lessons learned from other Information Management Group (IMG) initiated projects and other initiatives that relate to the EPR.

9. To ensure that appropriate confidentiality and security safeguards are built in and that the necessary data protection and medico-legal lessons are learned.

The brief

In line with many other large-scale contemporary IS projects (including CAPSA and Project A) it was decided to use the PRINCE methodology to manage the EPR project. As part of the first stage (initiation) the EPR Programme Board refined its objectives and began to identify the potential benefits of the EPR Project itself and of the effective EPR system it was intended to produce. At the same time, it started to consider the risks associated with the Project, identifying a number of hurdles at which the Project itself might fall, such as inability to find two appropriate demonstrator sites. It also recognized that important lessons might be learned from looking at previous attempts to introduce electronic patient record systems. Accordingly it commissioned the authors to conduct a study using the Systems Failures Approach. The formal brief for this was to identify the factors that are critical in ensuring the successful implementation of an electronic patient record (EPR) system in hospitals providing care to acutely ill patients.

It was agreed that the study would concentrate on the functions of the proposed system, the people who would use it and the environment in which it would be developed and used, and would assume that the EPR project itself would be well managed and would not of itself constitute a failure. It was also assumed that the EPR system, as designed, would carry out its intended functions and be robust and reliable and that sufficient funding/resources would be available for design and implementation and for the future running of the system.

The study

The study had two parts:

1. Systems failures analyses were made using published accounts of attempts to introduce clinical information systems.
2. The findings of the analyses and information gained from interviews with interested parties were used to look forward to the development and introduction of the EPR system with a view to predicting the risks associated with it.

A literature search revealed a number of accounts that were suitable for inclusion in the first part of the study. The criteria for inclusion were:

- hospital, as opposed to General Practice, setting;
- sufficient detail to allow analysis;
- the system being introduced was complex and had wide-ranging consequences.

The third of these posed the most problems. In terms of scope and sophistication the EPR system envisaged by the Programme Board was at the top of the range covered by the published accounts available.

The accounts used

Eight accounts were chosen:

1. The COSTAR V system at the Internal Medicine Department of Nebraska College of Medicine (Campbell *et al.*, 1989)
2. The mini-medical record system at the University of North Carolina Hospitals (Carey *et al.*, 1992)
3. The clinical information system at Columbia Presbyterian Medical Center (Clayton, Pulver & Hill, 1994)

4. The medical information system at the University of Virginia Medical Center (Massaro, 1993)
5. The Regenstrief MRS at 30 hospitals and clinics in the Indianapolis area (McDonald *et al.*, 1992)
6. The outpatient medical record system at Beth Israel Hospital (Rind & Safran, 1994)
7. OSCAR at Foothills Hospital, Calgary (Sears Williams, 1992)
8. COSTAR in the Outpatients Department of a 100-bed acute general hospital in the UK (Young, 1994).

Only a few of these will be summarized as examples. The first is Massaro's account of the introduction of a medical information system into a 700-bed teaching hospital at the University of Virginia, USA.

In 1981 a firm of management consultants recommended a programme of IT expansion at the hospital. This began with the successful introduction of a financial and accounting system and was to be followed by the installation of a medical information system (MIS) which would bring cost savings of $26.3 million over five years with a payback period of less than two years. From 1985 to 1987 basic administrative functions such as admission, discharge and transfer were computerized 'with no discernible impact on clinical practice'.

Between 1988 and 1991 the following were added in turn: on-line dietary and radiology orders; laboratory ordering and results retrieval; pharmacy; and major ancillaries and nursing procedure orders. But their introduction did not go smoothly. Delays built up and costs rose to almost three times the original estimates. Working relationships were also damaged: 'the project provoked a major confrontation between the medical staff and the hospital administration.' Cultural and behavioural problems emerged: 'the new system challenged basic institutional assumptions; it disturbed traditional patterns of conduct and forced people to modify established practice routines.' Valid criticisms of the quality and user-friendliness of the IT equipment were also often used as a 'surrogate for other agenda items related to the challenging of basic institutional assumptions and beliefs'.

The second account to be summarized is by Rind and Safran (1994) and looks at the outpatient medical record (OMR) system for outpatient care at Beth Israel Hospital in the USA. The system forms part of the hospital's large integrated clinical information system (there were more than 1400 terminals in total when the account was written) and was first used in 1989. It has been further developed since then (for example, the facility to write electronic notes was added towards the end of 1990) but four years after the initial introduction, paper records were still being kept alongside the electronic system. 'We currently print every note written in OMR and have it placed in the paper chart . . . significant handwritten charting continues.' This has led to significant printing problems, including finding sufficient space to house all the printers required.

Events surrounding the introduction of OMR were clearly far less dramatic than those described by Massaro (1993) but, nevertheless, barriers have been placed in its way. Indeed, Rind and Safran entitled their account 'Real and imagined barriers to an electronic medical record'.

OMR relies mainly on direct entry of data by clinicians. This proved to be less of a problem than expected: 'Clinicians are willing to keep extensive online problem lists and medication lists, and seem far more willing to type than had been predicted.' Data security and privacy provoked far more concern than was predicted and attempts to find solutions only led in turn to concerns that necessary access to information was being denied.

Analysis

Each of the eight accounts formed the basis for a comparison with the Formal System Model. It was recognized that each of the accounts was only partial, but as with many studies that are undertaken after the event, it was not practicable to flesh out the information with first-hand research. Nevertheless, by considering the results across eight different comparisons instead of relying on the results of individual comparisons, a powerful approach could be adopted that would enable the recurring themes to be identified.

By its inclusion in the selection that had been made, each of the accounts had been labelled a failure for the purposes of the study, with the extent and nature of the failure varying from case to case. For example, the COSTAR system described by Young had been introduced with the backing of seven consultants. One of them ceased to use it after his second clinic and another abandoned it part way through the first year. Several of its features were discontinued not long after introduction and although the remainder of the system ran for seven years until the hospital closed, only three of the consultants ever described it as useful and none of them asked for it to continue at the replacement hospital. The more sophisticated COSTAR V system described by Campbell *et al.* (1989) met with mixed reactions from physicians but was well received by nurses and clerical staff. However, although it was said to offer 'complete medical records features' and to have brought benefits such as greater efficiency for some aspects of patient care and improvements in physician performance with protocol care, Campbell *et al.* felt 'our results may point to a decrease in efficiency among the residents using COSTAR' and 'data from our time study suggest that ... benefits may not translate into faster or more efficient use of scheduled clinic time'.

In representing each account as a system that could be compared with the FSM, the perspective was that of an outsider with a brief to draw out lessons that could be applied elsewhere. For convenience, the FSM, which was introduced in Chapter 7, is reproduced again as Figure 9.1.

Comparison between the FSM and each of the eight systems representations produced sets of discrepancies and deficiencies that are summarized in Table 9.1.

Drawing together the results across the range of eight comparisons revealed five themes that were each common to a number of the accounts.

1. The subsystems which carried out the transformations tended not to have good links to the remainder of the systems or to the wider systems.
2. Ability to influence the environment appeared to be low while the disturbances, such as pressures for change, were high.
3. Decision-making subsystems tended to operate in isolation from the subsystems that carry out the transformations and, in some cases, were isolated from the wider system.
4. Expectations were not made known (at all levels).
5. Some resource problems existed.

Since one of the assumptions of the study was that the project would be properly resourced, the last of these themes was not considered further. In all the other main problem areas lack of involvement of key players and poor communications came across as particular causes for concern. Communication channels were ill-defined or non-existent and interfaces were too complex or otherwise inadequate.

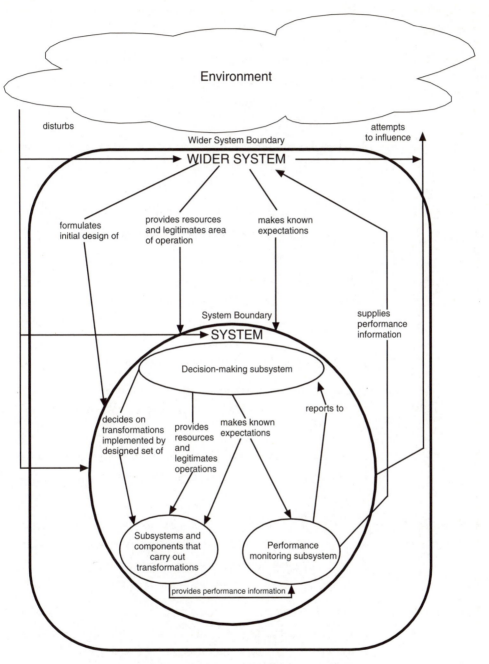

Figure 9.1 The Formal System Model

Table 9.1   Comparison between accounts and FSM

Account	Discrepancies and deficiencies
Campbell *et al.* (1989)	The decision-making subsystem within the system was deficient. For example, the effectiveness of reminder systems was limited by the sophistication of the decision rules that generated reminders.
Carey *et al.* (1992)	The wider system failed to provide sufficient resources; cost was seen as one of main barriers to a fully computerized system.
Clayton *et al.* (1994)	The design of the subsystems and components that carry out transformations within the system was deficient, resulting in low utilization by some physicians.
Massaro (1993)	All three of the necessary links from the wider system to the system were deficient. For some considerable time there was no decision-making subsystem. A team from the Computing Services Group devised the computer system and put it in place but had no decision-making authority.
McDonald *et al.* (1992)	The subsystems and components that carry out transformations were deficient, leading to data input problems.
Rind & Safran (1994)	There were problems with the formulation of the initial design of the system which presumably led to poor decision-making. Examples included printing difficulties and security and privacy problems.
Sears Williams (1992)	The link 'formulates initial design of' between the wider system and the system and that of 'makes known expectations' within the system were deficient, leading to the emergence of unexpected consequences from the design.
Young (1994)	The seven consultants who tried this system were never really part of the subsystem that carried out the transformations, even though they were, theoretically, the key users. In a sense these key people could not make their expectations known because they did not really have any. In the words of Young, 'They could not see much in the way of benefits.'

Over the accounts as a whole there was obvious and widespread evidence of in-group (management/administration) versus out-group (everyone else) problems and all the various groups – such as clinicians, managers, administrators and IT personnel – thought they knew best. There was little evidence of interdisciplinary teams being set up, and no evidence of them working. (The term 'interdisciplinary team' is being used here to denote a team with a common purpose rather than a group that merely provides a forum for consultation and discussion.) There were plenty of examples of conflict being allowed to grow, with some groups remaining unable or unwilling to buy into the systems, and very few instances in which conflict was ever really resolved. For example, in the account published by Massaro (1993), in-group versus out-group differences could be seen in the alteration of existing practices and clinicians, and the IT people were not able to combine to form a team capable of consensus decision-making. Conflict between the medics and the administrators reinforced the perception that the new system was a managerial initiative imposed from outside and had no real sponsorship from the medical community.

Conceptualizing an EPR system – modelling the future

For the second part of the study, the findings of the analyses of the published accounts, together with information gained from interviews with the project director and other interested parties, were used to look forward. First, an attempt was made to construct a systems map of the proposed EPR system and to use this to check understanding of the nature of the system. The final version, achieved after a number of iterations, is shown in Figure 9.2.

Formal System Models were then built at three different levels:

1. The highest level, i.e. the system level – a patient care system (see Figure 9.3).
2. The middle level, i.e. the subsystem level – a message system (see Figure 9.4).
3. The lowest level, i.e. the sub-subsystem level – a computer system (see Figure 9.5).

It was necessary to iterate between the three nested systems in order to check that the connections that would be necessary if the EPR system as a whole was to be capable of operating without failure had been considered.

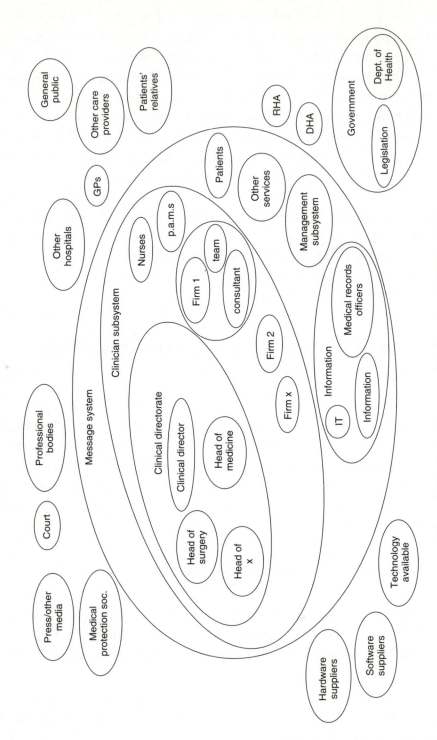

Figure 9.2 Systems map of the proposed EPR system

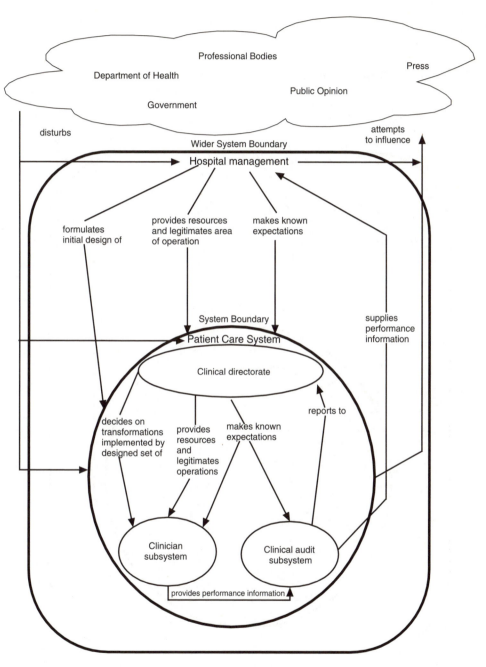

Figure 9.3 Model of a patient-care system

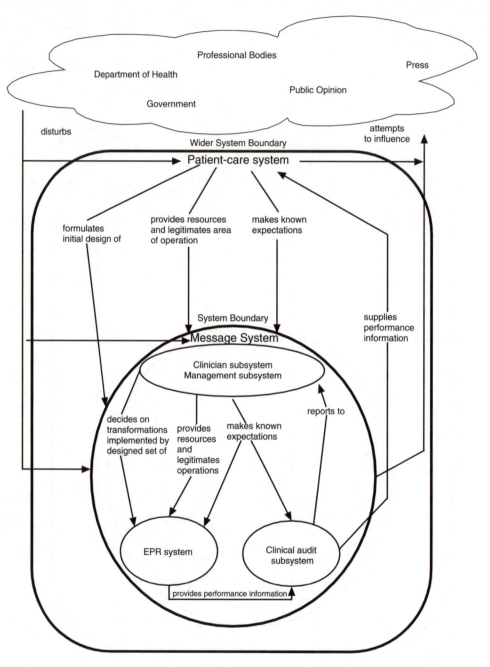

Figure 9.4   Model of a message system

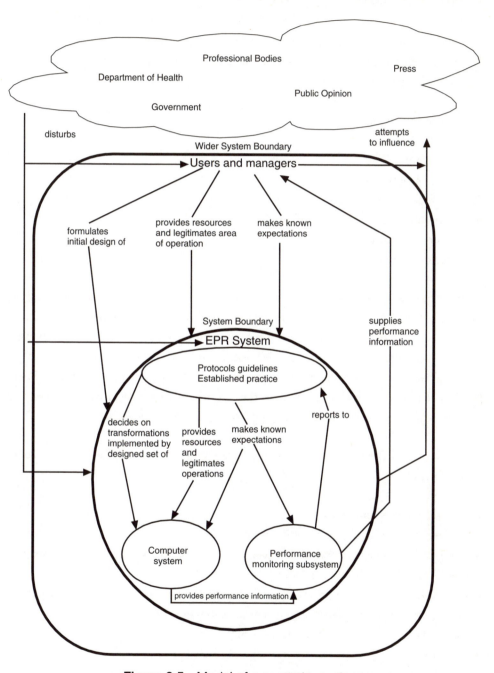

Figure 9.5 Model of a computer system

Findings and suggestions

The results from the study as a whole were brought together and reported to the Programme Board as a series of lessons. For ease of access these were grouped under eight subject headings as follows:

1. Reaction to change
2. Climate
3. Ownership
4. Threat or opportunity?
5. System and record design
6. User involvement in design and implementation
7. Choice of technology
8. Implementation.

Taking the lessons related to system and record design as an example, the analysis of the published accounts showed that false assumptions had frequently been made about how people worked, their information requirements, and the links that were needed within the systems. For example, custom and practice for routine tasks such as ordering tests was often different from the official procedures that had been laid down, but this 'flexibility', which is essential to the smooth operation of care procedures, had frequently not been built into the design of the computerized system.

The important issues for the EPR system selected under the heading 'system and record design' included:

- how the records will be used
- the level of detail required for different purposes
- the extent to which it will be necessary to be able to pick up patterns emerging over time
- information needed temporarily versus information required to be stored permanently, and whether there is always a clear distinction between the two
- the needs and preferences of individual clinicians
- team style
- the needs of different specialisms
- information needed for care of the patient as opposed to the treatment of disease
- treatment of patients with multiple problems if specialism-specific records are used.

It was pointed out that an effective design was likely to be one that would allow the data set or parts of it to be presented to different users in different forms, thus allowing for flexibility in the initial design and for different sets of expectations. For example, some users might regard it as essential to be able to view information by source, while others wish to view it by problem or by protocol.

The analysis showed that the question of standardization was important, with the balance of research evidence appearing to support the idea that standardization would improve the quality of records. Arguments in favour of standardization are that: it allows exchange of information; it prevents information overload by restricting the volume of information while not under-reporting; and it can reflect best practice. The problems that tend to be associated with standardization are that it requires the variations in terminology between individuals, between departments, between hospitals and so on to be ironed out and guidelines and protocols, standard definitions, structures and codes to be agreed before proofreads can be designed. Such agreements were not reached in many of the situations described in the accounts, and in some cases agreement had not even been sought.

Confidentiality, data security, and privacy were also important issues. In the UK the legal implications of the Data Protection Act 1984, the Access to Health Records Act 1990 and the guidelines issued by various bodies were important environmental influences, especially since medical negligence case law would hold an individual or group of clinicians responsible, rather than the system that provided the information. However, although it is an important area, the accounts tended to indicate that the issues of confidentiality, data security, and privacy were not as problematic as many perceive them to be.

In presenting the lessons, recommendations were made, where appropriate, to try to help to carry the project forward successfully. For instance, it was suggested that criteria for assessing the 'rightness' of the climate should be established before the demonstrator sites were chosen. Evidence from the published accounts suggested that lack of involvement, commitment and integration by key players, especially clinicians, had been an important feature in the failure of many electronic patient record systems, but there was a danger that demonstrator site selection would be largely determined by technical factors such as the computer systems already in place and the level of IT expertise available.

Conclusion

The client for the work described here felt that the report provided valuable criteria to help to identify two suitable hospitals to develop the demonstrators. The report was given to the project managers at each of the selected hospitals to use in project planning and the insights carried forward to contribute towards the selection of the criteria to be used to monitor the project.

However, as was stated in the introduction, the main purpose of this chapter has been to illustrate the process of using the Systems Failures Approach to look forward.

References

Campbell, J.R., Giver, N., Seelig, C.B., Greer, A.L., Patil, K., Wigton, R.S. & Tape, T. (1989) Computerized medical records and clinic function, *M.D. Computing*, 6: 282–287.

Carey, T.S., Thomas, D., Woolsey, A., Procter, R., Philbeck, M., Bower, G., Blish, C. & Fletcher, S. (1992) Half a loaf is better than waiting for the bread truck. *Archives of Internal Medicine*, 152: 1845–1849.

Clayton, P.D., Pulver, G.E. & Hill, C.L. (1994) Physician use of computers: is age or value the predominant factor? *AMIA*, 301–305.

McDonald, C.J. & Tierney, W.M. (1988) Computer-stored medical records. *JAMA*, 259: 3433–3440.

McDonald, C.J., Tierney, W.M., Overhage, J.M., Martin, D.K. & Wilson, G.A. (1992) The Regenstrief Medical Record System: 20 years of experience in hospitals, clinics, and neighbourhood health centers, *M.D. Computing*, 9: 206–217.

Massaro, T.A. (1993) Introducing physician order entry at a major academic medical center. *Academic Medicine*, 68: 20–30.

Patel, A.G., Mould, T. & Webb, P.J. (1993) Inadequacies of hospital medical records. *Annals of the Royal College of Surgeons of England*, 75: 7–9.

Rind, D.M. & Safran, C. (1994) Real and imagined barriers to an electronic medical record. *AMIA*, 74–78.

Royal College of Surgeons (1990) *Guidelines for Clinicians on Medical Records and Notes*. Royal College of Surgeons, London.

Sears Williams, L. (1992) Microchips versus stethoscopes: Calgary hospital, MDs face off over controversial computer system. *Canadian Medical Association Journal*, 147: 1534–1547.

Wrenn, K., Rodewald, L., Lumb, E. & Slovis, C. (1993) The use of structured, complaint-specific patient encounter forms in the emergency department. *Annals of Emergency Medicine*, 22: 805–812.

Young, D. (1994) Consultants' views on their use of a computer based medical record system. *Proceedings of Healthcare Computing 1994*, pp. 217–222.

Chapter 10

OTHER APPROACHES TO UNDERSTANDING IS FAILURES

Introduction

The main focus of this book has been the Systems Failures Approach. It has introduced the systems concepts that underpin the approach and shown how they can be brought together to investigate actual and potential information system failures.

The main purpose of this chapter is to look at other approaches that are available. They can be divided into three types. First, there are those that are essentially concerned with project management. Although some of these are aimed more at other types of projects such as engineering or construction, many are very suitable for IS projects. Secondly, there are approaches specifically developed for understanding IS failures. The third type covers approaches concerned with failures in general, regardless of whether they occur during the project phase, at implementation or within a well-established situation. As with project management approaches, not all of these are particularly applicable to the IS domain, but some are.

This chapter is not designed to provide an exhaustive survey of all the approaches, methods and techniques that can be used to gain understanding of information system failure, but it will cover at least one example of each of the three types identified above. In deciding which material to include, an attempt has been made to illustrate the range of what is available and reflect the amount of interest generated by particular approaches in the literature as well as including work which the authors have found to be particularly interesting, useful or informative.

Project management approaches relevant to IS failures

Critical factors

The term 'critical success factors' – defined as those factors that, if addressed, will improve the chances of project success to a significant extent – is used very widely in the project management literature. For example, Pinto and Slevin (1988, p. 67) identify 10 critical success factors for project implementation:

- *Project mission*   Initial clarity of goals and general directions.
- *Top management support*   Willingness of top management to provide the necessary resources and authority/power for project success.
- *Schedule/plans*   A detailed specification of the individual action steps for project implementation.
- *Client consultation*   Communication, consultation, and active listening to all impacted parties.
- *Personnel*   Recruitment, selection, and training of the necessary personnel for the project team.
- *Technical tasks*   Availability of the required technology and expertise to accomplish the specific technical action steps.
- *Client acceptance*   The act of 'selling' the final project to its ultimate intended users.
- *Monitoring and feedback*   Timely provision of comprehensive control information at each phase in the implementation process.
- *Communication*   The provision of an appropriate network and necessary data to all key actors in the project implementation.
- *Troubleshooting*   Ability to handle unexpected crises and deviations from plan.

Many other authors have published similar lists of factors, sometimes relating them to specific problem domains and types of activity (see, for example, Cleland & King, 1983; Morris & Hough, 1987; and Gowan & Mathieu, 1996). Belassi and Tukel (1996) have synthesized a number of lists to produce a framework (see Figure 10.1) that groups factors into four classes:

1. Factors related to the project
2. Factors related to the project manager and the team members
3. Factors related to the organization
4. Factors related to the external environment.

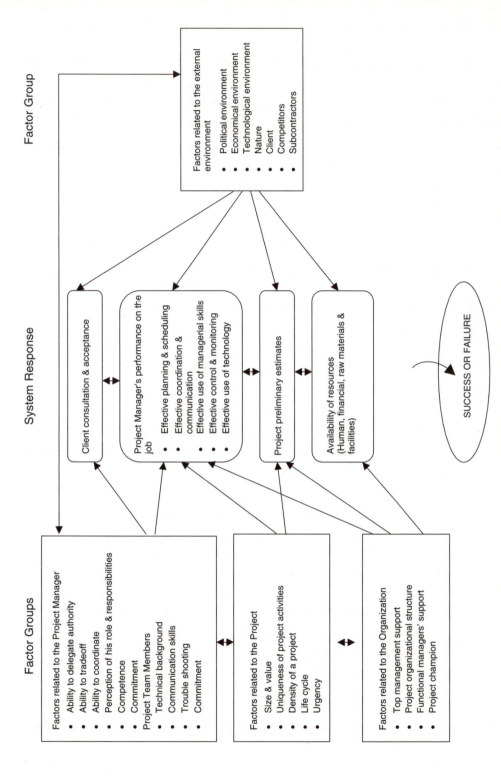

Figure 10.1 Critical success/failure factors in projects (Belassi & Tukel, 1996, p. 144)

The essence of this approach to understanding failure is to use the factors as a set of criteria for assessing project performance. One of the difficulties with this is knowing what would have constituted the 'optimal state' for any particular project. A second difficulty is deciding which set of factors to use. The many sets of factors that are available almost all fit neatly into Belassi and Tukel's classes but at the more detailed level there is only limited agreement among authors on the contents of the sets. Looking across the wide range available, it is easy to pick out the factors that are cited most frequently. These are:

- the importance of a project receiving support from senior management
- having clear and realistic objectives
- producing an efficient plan.

But although the majority of sets of criteria include at least one of these factors, very few include all three. One reason for this is the way in which each set of factors was developed. For example, Gowan and Mathieu (1996) determined their critical success factors 'through approximately twelve hours of interviews with seven individuals' who had worked together on the 'successful implementation of a fully automated FMS (flexible manufacturing system) located in the southeastern United States'. A different set of people or a different project experience may have given different results.

Belassi and Tukel (1996) point to an issue that also raises questions about the usefulness of the approach. They emphasize that the interrelationships between factors in different groups are as important as the individual factors:

> As can be seen from the figure [reproduced here as Figure 10.1], the groups are interrelated. A factor in one group can influence a factor in another group, and a combination of several factors from various groups which might lead to project failure. For instance, top management support is a factor related to an organization which can be affected by the general state of the economy. Similarly, the uniqueness of the project activities can affect the project manager's competence on the job. Lack of top management support together with the project manager's lack of competence on the job might lead to project failure.
>
> (Belassi & Tukel, 1996, p. 143)

The critical success factor approach does not, however, provide a mechanism for taking account of these interrelationships.

Approaches specifically developed for understanding IS failures

Factor approaches

A number of authors have taken a similar approach to the project management approach discussed above but have identified factors specifically associated with information systems. For example, Yap, Soh and Raman (1992) looked at computer-based information systems success factors in small businesses and concluded that six factors were important:

> consultant effectiveness
> vendor support
> duration of the organization's experience of computer-based information
>   systems
> sufficiency of financial resources
> level of chief executive's support
> user participation

(Yap, Soh & Raman, 1992, p. 608)

Caldeira and Ward (2002) have also taken a factor approach. After conducting in-depth case study research into IS/IT adoption and success in 12 Portuguese enterprises spread across four manufacturing industries (footwear, textiles, wine and the mould industry), they concluded that two factors had significant effects on levels of both adoption and success:

1. Management perspectives and attitudes towards IS/IT adoption and use
2. IS/IT competencies in terms of the IS/IT people and knowledge available

They labelled these two factors – both of which are aspects of the internal context of an organization – the determinant factors. They also identified two other sets of factors: situational factors that influenced the level of IS/IT adoption and use but did not explain the degree of IS/IT success achieved; and consequential factors that explained adoption and success but whose particular attributes appeared to depend upon, and result from, the nature and attributes of the determinant factors. In addition they discovered that a further set of factors that the literature suggested would be important were of no significance. All of these four sets of factors are shown in Table 10.1.

The determinant and consequential factors can be combined into an approach to understanding IS failure by using them as a set of criteria for assessing adoption and use.

Flowers (1996) has used a series of case studies to identify his set of factors. He has also turned the term 'critical success factor' on its head, referring instead to 'critical failure factors' which he defines as 'the crucial elements of a project that, when they are in a less than optimal state, will increase the chance that an IS project will either fail or at worst, become a disaster' (p. 157). After looking at failures associated with an on-line membership system for the Performing Right Society, a reservation system for American Airlines, the London Ambulance Service computerized despatch system, the London Stock Exchange TAURUS system and a trio of government IS systems, the factors he identified were:

Organizational context
Hostile culture
Poor reporting structures

Management of project
Over-commitment
Political pressures

Conduct of the project
Initiation stage
   Technology focused
   Lure of leading edge
Analysis and design phase
   Poor consultation
   Design by committee
   Technical 'fix' for management problem
Development phase
   Staff turnover
   Competency
   Communication
Implementation stage
   Receding deadlines
   Inadequate setting
   Inadequate user training.

(Flowers, 1996, p. 158)

Table 10.1 Suggested classification of factors associated with IS/IT adoption and success (Caldeira & Ward, 2002, p. 142)

	Situational	Determinant	Consequential	Not significant
1. *Internal context*	1.1 Financial resources	1.3 Management perspectives and attributes	1.5 Power relationships	1.7 Position of IS/IT manager
	1.2 Human resources	1.4 IS/IT competencies	1.6 User attributes	
2. *External context*	2.2 IS/IT external expertise available		2.1 IS/IT vendors' support	
	2.3 Quality of software available		2.4 Business pressure to adopt IS/IT	
3. *Process*			3.1 People involved	3.2 Frameworks and techniques used
			3.3 IS/IT Training	3.4 Stages followed in IS/IT development
4. *Context*	4.1 Type of IS/IT solutions available			4.3 Evaluation of IS/IT benefits
	4.2 IS/IT objectives			
	4.4 Time of IS/IT adoption			

Approaches such as these share the difficulties of the critical success factor approach to project management failures. For instance, Flowers' factors 'emerge from the case studies', so presumably there is no guarantee that the same factors would emerge from a different set of cases, particularly if he had looked at less complex or less sophisticated systems.

Larsen and Myers (1999, p. 398) draw attention to a further criticism that has been made: 'the factor approach tends to view implementation as a static process instead of a dynamic phenomenon, and ignores the potential for a factor to have varying levels of importance at different stages of the implementation process.'

Interaction approaches

The author most closely associated with the interaction perspective on IS failure is Markus (see, for example, Markus, 1983). The basis of her work is that 'the impacts of systems are not caused by system technology or by the people and organizations that use them but by the interaction between specific system design features and the related features of the system's organizational setting' (Markus, 1984, p. ix). A joint paper with Robey (Markus & Robey, 1983) sets out their version of the concept of organizational validity and identifies four levels of analysis that can be used to explain IS implementation problems.

> First, we view organizational validity not as a unitary concept but as a quality which can be assessed on at least four levels of analysis. Second, we view validity to be a property neither of systems nor of organizations, but of the match of fit between them. Third, we consider organizational validity to be a descriptive and relative concept rather than a normative and absolute one, with no simple connection between it and effective system use.
>
> (Markus & Robey, 1983, p. 205)

The first of the four levels of analysis for assessing organizational validity is the user-system level. They define organizational validity at this level as 'the degree of fit between users' psychological characteristics and system design attributes' in terms of 'users' motivations or cognitive styles' (p. 209). The second level is the structure-system level, concerned with 'the match between the structural characteristics of an organization and different system design attributes' (p. 209). The third is the power-system level:

> While an information system might validly fit the organization task and users' needs and cognitive styles, it might be resisted because it causes a redistribution of power unacceptable to those losing power. Thus, organizational validity can also be defined in terms of the distribution of power within an organization; a system can be said to be invalid to the extent that it embodies a power distribution at odds with that existing in the organizational context of use. (p. 210)

The fourth level is the environment-system level. This is concerned with 'the fit between the system design characteristics and the environment of the organization in which it is used' (p. 211).

This approach has been designed to understand failures where there has been resistance within an organization to an information system that is being introduced. Pliskin *et al.* (1993) provide one example of its application, and at the same time suggest a fifth level of analysis, the culture-system level, which is concerned with 'the fit between the organizational culture presumed in the design of the system and the actual organizational culture in the implementing organization' (p. 146). They collected data for their analysis through textual analysis of documents, questionnaires, interviews and direct observation, and then, at each level of analysis, contrasted assumptions made by the company that had been contracted to supply an employee evaluation system about its client's organization against the realities at the client organization. They found a lack of fit between the system and the organization at all except the user-system level and concluded that 'growing resistance [to the system] was a rational response to a gap at four out of five levels of organizational analysis' (p. 149).

In considering whether this approach is an appropriate mechanism for understanding IS failure, it is important to note Markus and Robey's own words of caution against trying to use the concept of organizational validity normatively:

> ...the hypothesis that organizationally invalid systems, that is, systems mis-matched to their organizational context of use on any or all of four dimensions, are more difficult to implement than valid ones is intuitively pleasing, since the

introduction of an invalid system requires change from existing organizational thinking and behavior patterns. It is by no means certain, however, that validity will lead to effective use or invalidity to ineffective use. The success of the outcome will clearly depend, at least in part, on how effective and successful were the thinking and behavior patterns which the information system did or did not match. Thus, an organizationally valid information system might be easily installed but fail to produce any significant benefits because it merely automates inefficient organizational rules of thumb. Or, a highly invalid system might generate enormous resistance as it is installed, yet lead to a major long-run improvement in organizational effectiveness. Therefore, while we may point out ways in which the organizational validity of an information system can be increased, because we are using the concept descriptively, we intend no simple prescriptions about the wisdom of doing so.

(Markus & Robey, 1983, p. 206)

Interpretive approaches

Interpretive approaches are derived from the social sciences and are based on the belief that reality is socially constructed and can be understood by interpreting data sources, such as transcripts of interviews, with the use of methods such as meaning condensation, meaning categorization, narrative structuring and hermeneutic meaning interpretation.

The attempts to apply interpretive approaches to understanding IS failures that have been reported in the literature use the hermeneutical circle as the main device for gaining understanding. Information is gathered about a failure situation, the analyst then looks for apparent absurdities in the situation and questions how a sensible person could behave in that way. When an answer is found the analyst looks again at the situation and develops a new understanding of it, then continues around this loop until the meaning of the situation has been extracted.

One approach of this type has been developed by Davis *et al.* (1992). It combines use of the hermeneutical circle with a framework for analysis that is based upon two premises: 'an information system is a *social system that uses information technology*'; and IS success or failure cannot be explained in terms of either the information technology alone or the social system alone. Accordingly, the framework has two dimensions, one concerned with the social system, and the other concerned with the technical

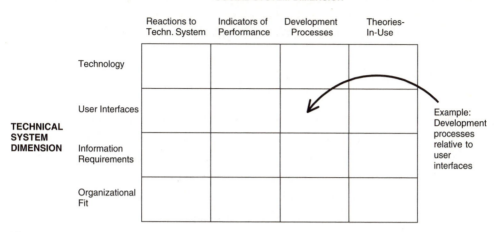

Figure 10.2 Two dimensional matrix for diagnosing an information system failure (Davis *et al.*, 1992, p. 298)

aspects. As shown in Figure 10.2, each dimension is divided into four to give 16 areas of 'potentially useful data for a failure diagnosis'. The divisions of the social system dimension are:

1. Reactions of people to the technical system.
2. Indicators of technical system performance meaningful to the social system showing the extent to which the technical system contributes or fails to contribute to the goals of the social system and the extent to which it satisfies or respects the constraints faced by the social system.
3. Development processes used to design, develop and implement the technical system.
4. 'Theories-in-use' of those involved in building the technical system.

The divisions of the technical system dimension are:

1. The technology itself, including the hardware, software and related technology.
2. The interfaces between the users and the technology.
3. The capacity of the new system to support users in terms of meeting pre-existing requirements and any new capabilities that were promised.
4. The fit between the technical system and the politics and culture of the organization.

The first stage of Davis *et al.*'s approach is to gather data on the IS failure using interviews, observation and written sources and then classify it using the 16 cells of the framework. Any apparent anomalies or indications of seemingly irrational behaviour in the data in the completed matrix are then noted and form the input to the interpretive process. The purpose of the interpretation is to resolve the anomalies or irrationalities.

Davis *et al.* explain this interpretive process thus:

> The hermeneutical circle may turn the observer's attention to certain aspects of the IS failure that earlier were ignored. These aspects may be 'missing pieces' in the puzzle which the IS failure presents. Facts and perceptions already observed and recorded as data in the matrix may emerge to hold new significance. A new round of observations might even be needed to collect additional data. In this sense, interpretation guides observation, just as observation guides interpretation. . . . the hermeneutical circle ties together the data – the facts and perceptions – that have been recorded throughout the sixteen different cells of the two-dimensional matrix. An important, additional point is that the observer may choose to extend the hermeneutical circle to the context outside of the immediate 'text'.
>
> (Davis *et al.*, 1992, p. 304)

To explain their approach further, Davis *et al.* use the introduction of FAS, a system for managing personnel data, into the management school of a major US university. One of the items they noted in cell C1 of the framework was 'lack of appropriate development included the fact that key stakeholders such as faculty [members] who are experts in technical design were not involved in the development of FAS'. They regarded this as an anomaly and therefore used the hermeneutical circle to try to relate it to other behaviours that had been inputted into the framework. Their interpretation was as follows:

> The system builders' noninvolvement of key stakeholders emerges as sensible for them, considering their theories-in-use (the fourth component of the social system dimension). These include a theory-in-use which views the role of management as responsible for design decision (an 'only-top-management-as-user' theory-in-use) . . . Such a view leads naturally to the exclusion of other stakeholders. The interpretation, therefore, focuses attention on the consequences of the theory-in-use.
>
> (Davis *et al.*, 1992, p. 304)

One of the criticisms that has been directed at Davis *et al.*'s approach is that the social system dimension is too narrow. Mitev (1996) claims that:

> The social system dimension must include the larger social and political processes through which the interests of different social groups interact with one another and with the technology (Robinson, 1994). This implies that macrosocial and historical factors must be investigated as well as the multi-causal relationship more immediately involved in failure (Lyytinen & Hirschheim, 1987).
>
> (Mitev, 1996, p. 9)

The issue of historical factors is raised in a paper by Myers (1994, p. 189). In many ways he takes a similar approach to that of Davis *et al.* but links his work specifically to the critical hermeneutics of the philosophers Gadamer and Ricoeur and works straight from a case study-type text rather than classifying the information prior to interpretation. But although Myers takes his readers through the analysis of a failed attempt by the New Zealand Education Department to implement a centralized payroll system, he does not codify his approach to an extent that would necessarily allow others to copy it with any high degree of confidence. This is perhaps not surprising in that interpretive approaches, and indeed many other qualitative approaches, are deliberately subjective and relativist.

The triangle of dependences approach

The triangle of dependences approach (Figure 10.3) was developed by Sauer (1993) as 'a tool to aid analysis of the information systems process' (p. 64). He explains it thus:

> Each relationship represented by a side of the triangle [see Figure 10.3] is subject to a variety of influences. These influences make some aspects of the process uncontrollable but at the same time they provide scope for managing other aspects. Under the standard organisational constraints and contingencies the information systems process will be flawed and will produce flawed systems. However, flaws alone do not constitute failure. Rather, it is the role of flaws in diminishing level of support that links them to failure.
>
> (Sauer, 1993, p. 64)

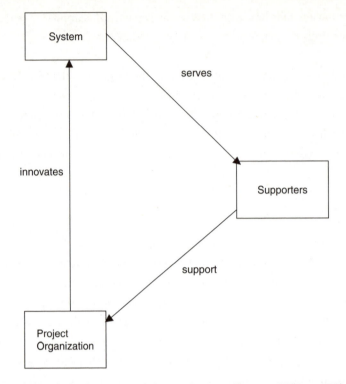

Figure 10.3   Triangle of dependences (Sauer, 1993, p. 56)

The Project Organization in the triangle is

> the group of people who at a particular point in time are occupied with the process of developing, implementing, operating or maintaining a given system. Typically those people recognized by other organizational actors as chiefly responsible for these various processes constitute the project organization. . . . Users involved in development full-time may still not be part of the project organization because they remain independent.
>
> (Sauer, 1993, pp. 11–12)

The Supporters fall into three categories: funders; fixers; and power-brokers. The funders provide resources, including 'information where it is more like a capital resource than a consumable'. Fixers, who may or may not be part of the project organization, 'manage strategic contingencies, control important decisions, and provide information with a shorter lifespan' (p. 57). Power-brokers wield influence over those

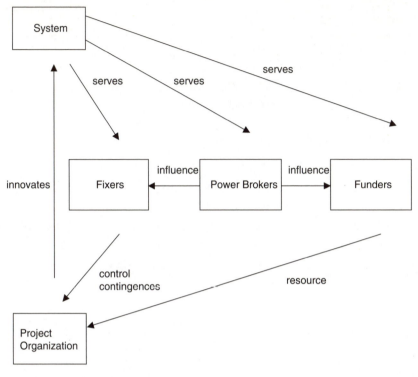

Figure 10.4 Expanded triangle of dependences (Sauer, 1993, p. 100)

who control funds and contingencies. These groups are shown in the expanded triangle of dependencies (Figure 10.4).

Analysis using the triangle of dependences approach proceeds as follows. First, all the available information about the situation is drawn together and the information systems process is divided into the stages shown in Table 10.2. Each stage is then investigated in turn, looking at effects of context and the effect of evaluations on decisions. The effects of context are evaluated on six dimensions: cognitive limits; technical process; environment; politics; history; and structure. For example, when looking at the effects of context on the initiation phase of a system to automate personnel and establishments record processing for the whole of the Australian Public Service (the project was initiated in 1970 and abandoned in 1981) Sauer made the evaluation shown in Table 10.3. Table 10.4 summarizes the decision-making processes, showing the effect the evaluation processes of the initiation phase had on support. Based on these two analyses of each stage, lessons are drawn across the information systems process as a whole.

Table 10.2 Stages of the process (Sauer, 1993, p. 69)

Stage	Component substage
Initiation	Detection of performance gap
	Formation of attitudes
	Development of proposal
	Strategic decision-making
Development	Development of abstract system
	Development of concrete system
	Establishment of project infrastructure
Implementation	Introduction of concrete system to operational and organizational context
Operation	Operation, maintenance and enhancement

Table 10.3 Effects of context on the initiation phase (Sauer, 1993, p. 254)

Contextual factor	Effect on innovation process
Cognitive limits	Normal uncertainties in the design
Technical process	Unproblematic
Environment	Relatively favourable. Technology changing rapidly
Politics	No specific power plays
History	No specific precedents
Structure	Lack of streamlined decision process

Sauer points to the main limitation of his approach:

> The focus ... [is] on the project organization... The conclusion that information systems failure may sometimes be unavoidable by the project organization highlights the limits to the project organization's abilities. Extending a point made by Markus (1984), there are some tasks user managers rather than systems analysts may not be able to do and which must be left to supporters. The failure of supporters to help can be very debilitating.
>
> (Sauer, 1993, p. 321)

Table 10.4   The effect of evaluations on decisions about support (Sauer, 1993, p. 255)

Evaluation/Decisions	Date	Evaluation	Effect on support
Feasibility study	Nov. 1971	+ve	Led to Board decision to consult further
Public Service Board	Feb. 1972	Decision	Decision to consult widely
Consultants	Sep. 1972	+ve	Positive effect on Board and IDC on ADP
Departments	May–Dec. 1972	Mostly +ve	Encouraged Board to fund Cabinet submission
Public Service Board	Mar. 1973	Decision	Board authorizes funding for Cabinet submission and initial establishment of project
IDC on ADP	May 1973	+ve	Prerequisite of Cabinet submission
Committee of Officials	Jan. 1974	+ve	Prerequisite of Cabinet support
Staff Associations	Late 1973	+ve	Little effect. Board proceeds in absence of negative responses
Cabinet	Feb. 1974	Decision	Funds approved for hardware and software

Context specific approaches

A factor-based approach can also be applied and refined in specific types of situation and combined with another approach. Heeks (2002) has been concerned over a number of years with the significant number of failures in IS projects in developing countries. He tries to move beyond a simple factor approach to a framework based in part upon systems ideas and contingency theory. The essence of the framework is an analysis of the gap that exists between the 'current realities' and the 'design conceptions' of the information system on seven dimensions of: information; technology; processes; objectives, values and motivations; staffing and skills; management and structures; and other resources. These seven dimensions result from extensive case study analysis and lead Heeks to the following generalizations about the gaps that are particular to developing world information systems:

Information: formal, quantitative information stored outside the human mind is valued less in developing countries.

Technology: the technological infrastructure (telecommunications, networks, electricity) is more limited and/or older in the developing countries.

Processes: work processes are more contingent in developing countries because of the more politicised and inconstant environment.

Objectives, values and motivations: developing countries are reportedly more likely to have cultures that value kin loyalty, authority, holism, secrecy, and risk aversion.

Staffing and skills: developing countries have a more limited local skills base in a wide range of skills. This includes IS/ICT skills of systems analysis and design, implementation skills, and operation-related skills including computer literacy and familiarity with the Western languages that dominate computing. It also includes a set of broader skills covering the planning, implementation and management of IS initiatives.

Management and structures: developing country organisations are more hierarchical and more centralised.

Other resources: developing countries have less money. In addition, the cost of ICTs is higher than in industrialised countries whereas the cost of labour is less.

(Heeks, 2002, p. 8)

Heeks readily acknowledges that there are many exceptions to these stereotypes but he argues that they go someway towards explaining why IS applications and the underlying assumptions developed in more industrialized contexts may not always readily transfer to developing contexts.

General failure approaches relevant to IS failures

Failures as organizational phenomena

One particularly significant contribution to the literature which looks at failures as organizational phenomena can be found in the work of the late Barry Turner (Peters & Turner, 1976; Turner, 1979). The approach used by Turner (and, indeed, others) was to try to identify underlying or common themes that can be found again and again in different situations. The method he used to try to identify these themes took the form of a systematic and scholarly enquiry into a small but carefully selected sample of disasters. Using the official enquiry reports of three contemporary accidents, he undertook a comparative study of the following disasters:

1. The 1966 Aberfan tip disaster in which a portion of the waste tip of the local colliery slid down into the village of Aberfan and in so doing killed 144 people, 116 of whom were children in the village school.
2. The Hixon level crossing accident in which a train hit a large road transporter in 1968. The incident occurred at a new type of automatic level crossing where the times allowed for the warning period were insufficient for such a slow-moving transporter.
3. The Summerland fire at a newly built holiday leisure complex on the Isle of Man. The complex was of a novel acrylic-covered steel-frame design. 3000 people were inside the building at the time and 50 of them died in the rapidly spreading fire.

Turner concluded that although the details of the three failures were very different, there were eight classes of similarity among them and, interestingly, despite their lack of any connection with IS, all the classes, with the possible exception of the sixth, have relevance to the study of IS failures. The eight classes are:

1. Rigidities in perception and beliefs in organizational settings. Within an organization there will, to some extent, be a similarity of approach and a distinctive culture which distinguishes it from others, and which may contribute to its success. Turner argues that this commonality may also lead to narrowed perceptions and may restrict the decision-making of the organization. One example he quotes from the Aberfan Tribunal report illustrates how the colliery workers were concerned with coal production and not the dangers associated with the disposal of the waste products. This common perception seemed to make them oblivious to the dangers associated with the tip.

> We found that many witnesses, not excluding those who were intelligent and anxious to assist us, had been oblivious of what lay before their eyes. It did not enter their consciousness. They were like moles being asked about the habits of birds.

2. *Decoy problems.* Difficulties and potential problems may be identified and dealt with, but these often turn out not to be the ones that lead to the accident. For example, there was concern about tipping at Aberfan, but when the tipping was stopped the danger was assumed to have passed even though the tip itself was still present.

3. *Organizational exclusivity.* The employees of an organization will be expert in its activities, therefore they may devalue the concerns expressed by outsiders.

4. *Information difficulties.* There is a tendency for any accident report to identify poor information and communications as contributory factors and to recommend better communications. Turner went beyond this to analyse the necessary features of secure communication and the potential for failure at various points. (Communications is dealt with in Chapter 4 of this book.)

5. *The involvement of 'strangers', especially on complex 'sites'.* The concept of a site arises from a physical situation which, as well as being designed for one purpose, has features and characteristics that make it apparently suitable for other purposes. Turner identifies strangers as another common feature. These are groups who are outside the immediate control and influence of an organization. They may be the general public or employees of other organizations, but briefing them and being certain of their levels of knowledge is problematic. As a simple example, a tractor may be designed for farm work, but to a young child it may look like an attractive piece of play equipment. The child then is a stranger on this site.

Strangers have been defined as people who have access to a part of a system, not necessarily legally, and who cannot be adequately briefed about the situation because they are not sufficiently clearly identified to enable training to take place, or because the 'keepers of the system' do not have sufficient influence over them to be informed.

A site is a concrete subsystem, the components of which have additional properties to those required by the system (Peters & Turner, 1976).

6. *Failure to comply with regulation.* Turner identifies the inadequacy of existing regulations and the failure to revise and control the implementation of regulations.

7. *Minimizing emergent dangers.* Turner demonstrates a consistent pattern of under-estimating the dangers as they become apparent. This pattern stretches from the initial recognition of the possibility of a hazard through to the first signs of the accident itself and a reluctance to call immediately for help. Even when the full potential of the danger is recognized the action taken may be inadequate and defensive. Turner quotes the British Railways fiat 'vehicles must not become immobilised on these crossings' as an example of the latter.

8. *Nature of the recommendations: well-structured problems.* A final aspect of Turner's findings was that the recommendations of the inquiry were concerned with the avoidance of similar incidents. However, in the main the recommendations assumed that the problem had been identified and, as he puts it, 'structured', whereas the situation faced by the participants in the disaster had been ill-structured. This eighth point is included for completeness, although it is really a commentary on the learning process associated with failures rather than on the failures themselves.

Returning to the Systems Failures Approach

In this book, application of the Systems Failures Approach has been confined to actual and potential information system failures. However, its use is not confined to the IS field. Its origins lie in the study of catastrophes. Examples of these can be found in Bignell, Peters and Pym (1977). They include the Aberfan disaster, as also studied by Turner (*op. cit.*), and events such as the Ronan Point collapse in 1968 when a gas explosion on the eighteenth floor of a system-built tower block caused the entire corner of the block to fall to the ground. Since then, topics looked at using the approach include accidents (e.g. Powell, 1987), construction projects (e.g. Bignell & Fortune, 1984), emergency planning (e.g. Horlick-Jones, 1990; Brearley, 1991), science education in primary schools (Fortune, Peters & Rawlinson-Winder, 1993), command and control in policing (Pearce & Fortune, 1995) and industrial disasters (e.g. Fortune & Peters, 1995).

One of the interesting questions raised by the wide range of applicability of the Systems Failures Approach and some of the other approaches covered in this chapter is whether IS failures are different from other failures.

A study by a working group from The Royal Academy of Engineering and The British Computer Society (2004) sought to 'improve the understanding of how complex IT projects differ from other engineering projects', but concluded:

> There is a broad reluctance to accept that complex IT projects have many similarities with major engineering projects and would benefit from greater application of well established engineering and project management procedures. (p. 4)

and

> It is time for the IT industry to recognise collectively the engineering content of their work and to embrace the discipline and professionalism associated with traditional branches of engineering. (p. 33)

Looking at this cynically one could, of course, draw parallels between the lists of failures with which this book began (for example, the Defence Stores Management Solution project brought to a halt in 2002 after £130 million had been spent, and the delays costing £12 million in processing British passport applications following the introduction in 1999 of the Passport Agency's new system) and high-profile construction failures that were happening around the same time (such as the London Millennium Bridge that opened late and over budget, stayed open for three days and then closed again for two years while £5 million was spent to stop it wobbling, and the Millennium Dome at Greenwich with final construction costs of £332.3 million compared with an official estimate made in June 1997 of £198 million).

Elsewhere, however, it is suggested that information systems projects may have particular characteristics that cause them to fail. For example, Morris argues that:

> IT projects do indeed pose a particular class of management difficulty. The essence of this difficulty is the way that information technology is so intimately bound into its organizational contexts. As a result, issues of organizational effectiveness and user involvement are both more complex and

more prominent in IT projects than they are in most other project industries. This puts much greater emphasis on the tasks of project definition and user involvement in IT than in other project situations.

(Morris, 1996, p. 323).

It is certainly the case that taking account of users' and some other stakeholders' needs is particularly problematical where IS design is concerned. As Flowers (1996, p. 87) says:

The history of IS usage in organizations is littered with examples of systems that were either never used or were under-used because of poor consultation. This danger is recognized within the Inquiry Report [into the failure of the London Ambulance Service computerized despatch system] which states that any future system '… must have total ownership by management and staff'.

It was also seen in some of the accounts used in the analysis reported in Chapter 9 of this book.

In order to provide system developers with tools that will enable them to cope with the problems alluded to above by Morris (1996), White (2003) has developed a project-specific form of the Formal System Model and devised a schema to assist in ensuring that all project stakeholders and environmental risks are successfully identified at the start of a project.

The project-specific form of the Formal System Model is shown in Figure 10.5. It incorporates all the systems concepts and other features, as discussed in Chapter 7, but aims specifically to assist project managers to predict and manage project risk. It can be used at the design stage of a project's life cycle to build a model of the proposed project to ensure that all necessary components have been identified, that possible communication links have been investigated, and that feedback mechanisms have been put in place. If the need for changes to the project plan are indicated, it can then be revisited to ensure that factors critical to the project's outcome have not been overlooked.

As long ago as 1980, Burnett and Youker advocated the importance of analysing a project's environment and developed a process called 'stakeholder mapping' to identify the people or groups who had a stake in a project. This work was further developed

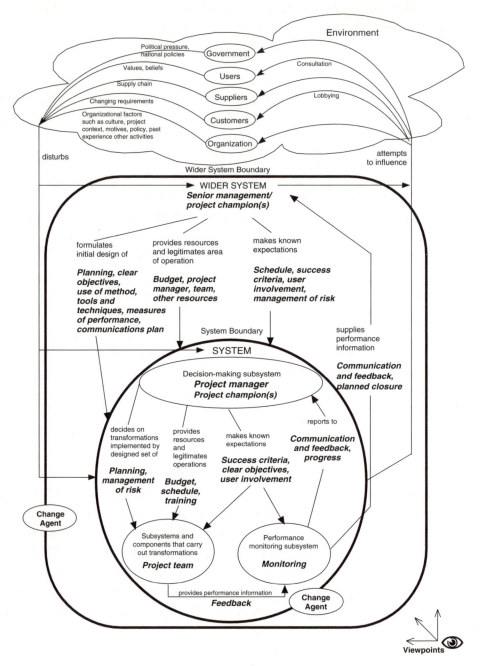

Figure 10.5 Project-specific form of the Formal System Model (White, 2003)

by Archibald (1992) who put forward the idea of undertaking systematic scanning of a project's environment to identify key actors and factors that might be crucial to its success. The schema shown in Figure 10.6 builds on their work. It allows viewpoints to be considered and the project's environment to be scanned at the feasibility stage to identify factors that could affect the outcomes of the project. Each factor can then be assessed for its level of risk and strategies developed to reduce or deal with any risks identified. The schema can then be used in conjunction with the project-specific form of the Formal System Model to ensure that all stakeholders' views and environmental risks are identified at the start of a project and allowed for where necessary. From thenceforward it can be used on a regular basis to alert those involved in the project to changes that are taking place as the project proceeds.

The risk-related role of the schema means that it can support the National Audit Office's risk management requirements as set out in its report *Supporting Innovation: Managing Risk in Government Departments* (National Audit Office, 2000a). These are summarized in other NAO reports, including the cancellation of the Benefits Payment Card project, as follows:

Setting clear objectives: defining aims and objectives which can be used as a basis for identifying risks to the project and to the purchaser's wider business and reputation.

Risk identification: listing each risk that could conceivably occur, and recording them for future management in a risk register or other control system. Risk registers are a common feature of successful Information Technology projects.

Risk assessment: assigning to each risk an estimate of the probability of it occurring and the impact on the project if it does; and

Risk mitigation, monitoring and control: including the allocation of each risk to a named individual or entity with the responsibility and authority to manage it, the selection by risk managers of options to deal with unacceptable risk, and regularly monitoring identified risks and the effectiveness of the actions taken

(National Audit Office, 2000b, pp. 40–41)

Viewpoints

 Viewpoint 1:
Users - including their demands/expectations and the effect of the project on their values, beliefs, behaviour, commitment, attitude to risk.

 Viewpoint 2:
Those affected by project who receive no direct benefit - including any changes to their physical/material state that could arise from the project or from any changes in the behaviour of the project users.

 Viewpoint 3:
Project team - including the effect any changes to working conditions may have on the team's morale/families.

 Viewpoint 4:
Organization in which the project is placed - including the effect of project on overall business plan and any other changes to the business, sales and other opportunities, staff relations, staff expectations, possible redundancies.

 Viewpoint 5:
Supporters - to include partners, contractors, sub-contractors, suppliers, financiers, insurers, clients, customers.

 Viewpoint 6:
Opponents - to include competition, pressure groups, campaigns, public opinion, those resisting change.

 Viewpoint 7:
Beneficiaries or Customers - to include those who are affected by project and who do receive direct benefit but who do not make use of any project outcome.

FINANCIAL/ECONOMIC SYSTEM
World/national economy, world/national/local banks, foreign exchange rates, interest rates, inflation, markets, competition, *resource costs, project related borrowing*

SOCIO/CULTURAL SYSTEM
Beliefs, needs, behaviour, ethics, human error, attitude to risk, incentives, press & media

POLITICAL/LEGAL SYSTEM
National/local policies/laws/rules unions, taxes, safety issues, *public relations*

ORGANIZATIONAL SYSTEM
Structure/culture of parent organization, staff loyalty, other organizational activities, past experience, partners, contractors, suppliers, client/customer demands/expectations

INFRASTRUCTURAL SYSTEM
National/local transport/roads national/local utilities, national/ local health/education provision, Internet/WAN/LAN, other established communication paths

TECHNOLOGICAL SYSTEM
Technical knowledge/experience, technical advances, *applicable/available technology, research, project related research*

PHYSICAL SYSTEM
Geology, geography, soil conditions, *land erosion, drainage, weather, pests, diseases*

Environmental Sweep

KEY TO ENVIRONMENTAL SWEEP:
Words in regular text = system should appreciate
Words in italics = system should appreciate, may be possible for system to influence
Words that are underlined = system should appreciate, may be possible for system to influence and attempt to control

Figure 10.6   The schema – viewpoints and environmental sweep (White, 2003)

Conclusion

The major part of this book has been an explanation of an approach to the analysis of failure that has been developed over a long period and has been re-examined and revised to ensure that it is well-suited to cope with the particular demands of IS. We believe that the reflective approach inherent in the study of failure has much to offer organizations facing increasingly turbulent environments. It is our hope that this book will contribute to the wider understanding and analysis of IS and other failures, and that it will encourage others to be less reticent about admitting to failures and sharing the results of their experiences and analyses with others so that the same types of mistake do not continue to be made over and over again.

References

Archibald, R.D. (1992) *Managing High-Technology Programs and Projects*. John Wiley & Sons, Chichester.

Belassi, W. & Tukel, O.I. (1996) A new framework for determining critical success/failure factors in projects. *International Journal of Project Management*, 14: 141–151.

Bignell, V. & Fortune, J. (1984) *Understanding Systems Failures*. Manchester University Press, Manchester.

Bignell, V., Peters, G. & Pym, C. (1977) *Catastrophic Failures*. Open University Press, Milton Keynes.

Brearley, S.A. (1991) High level management and disaster. In A.Z. Keller & H.C. Wilson (eds) *Emergency Planning in the 1990s*. British Library/Technical Communications, Letchworth.

Burnett, N.R. & Youker, R. (1980) *Analyzing the project environment*, EDI Course Notes CN-848, World Bank, Washington, DC.

Caldeira, M.M. & Ward, J.M. (2002) Understanding the successful adoption and use of IS/IT in SMEs: An explanation from Portuguese manufacturing industries. *Information Systems Journal*, 12: 121–152.

Cleland, D.I. & King, W.R. (1983) *Systems Analysis and Project Management*. McGraw-Hill, New York.

Davis, G.B., Lee, A.S., Nickles, K.R., Chatterjee, S., Hartung, R. & Wu, Y. (1992) Diagnosis of an information system failure. *Information & Management*, 23: 293–318.

Flowers, S. (1996) *Software Failure: Management Failure*. John Wiley & Sons, Chichester.

Fortune, J. & Peters, G. (1995) *Learning from Failure*. John Wiley & Sons, Chichester.

Fortune, J., Peters, G. & Rawlinson-Winder, L. (1993) Science education in English and Welsh primary school: A systems study. *Journal of Curriculum Studies*, 25: 359–369.

Gowan, J.A. & Mathieu, R.G. (1996) Critical factors in information system development for a flexible manufacturing system. *Computers in Industry*, 28: 173–183.

Heeks, R. (2002) *Failure, success and improvisation of information systems projects in developing countries*. Development Informatics Working Paper 11, Institute for Development Policy and Management, University of Manchester, Manchester.

Horlick-Jones, T. (1990) *Acts of God? An Investigation Into Disasters*. EPI Centre, London.

Larsen, M. & Myers, M. (1999) When success turns to failure: A package-driven process re-engineering project in the financial services industry. *Journal of Strategic Information Systems*, 8: 395–417.

Lyytinen, K. & Hirschheim, R. (1987) Information systems failures: A survey and classification of the empirical literature. In P. Zorkoczy (ed.) *Oxford Surveys in Information Technology*. Oxford University Press, Oxford, pp. 257–309.

Markus, M.L. (1983) Power, politics and MIS implementation. *Communications of the ACM*, 26: 430–444.

Markus, M.L. (1984) *Systems in Organizations: Bugs and Features*. Pitman, Boston.

Markus, M.L. & Robey, D. (1983) The organizational validity of management information systems. *Human Relations*, 36: 203–226.

Mitev, N.N. (1996) More than a failure? The computerized reservation systems at French Railways. *Information Technology & People*, 9: 8–19.

Morris, P.W.G. & Hough, G.H. (1987) *The Anatomy of Major Projects*. John Wiley & Sons, Chichester.

Morris, P.W.G. (1996) Project management: Lessons from IT and non-IT projects. In M.J. Earl (ed.) *Information Management, the Organizational Dimension*. Oxford University Press, Oxford, pp. 321–366.

Myers, M.D. (1994) A disaster for everyone to see: an interpretive analysis of a failed project. *Accounting, Management and Information Technology*, 4: 185–201.

National Audit Office (2000a) *Supporting Innovation: Managing Risk in Government Departments*. The Stationery Office, London.

National Audit Office (2000b) *The Cancellation of the Benefits Payment Card Project*. The Stationery Office, London.

Pearce, T. & Fortune, J. (1995) Command and control in policing – a systems assessment of the Gold, Silver, Bronze structure. *Journal of Contingencies and Crisis Management*, 3: 181–187.

Peters, G. & Turner, B.A. (1976) *Catastrophe and its Preconditions*. Open University Press, Milton Keynes.

Pinto, J.K. & Slevin, D.P. (1988) Critical success factors across the project life cycle. *Project Management Journal*, XIX: 67–75.

Pliskin, N., Romm, T., Lee, A.S. & Weber, Y. (1993) Presumed versus actual organizational culture: Managerial implications for implementation of information systems. *The Computer Journal*, 36: 143–152.

Powell, D. (1987) A study of the Seer Green Railway accident (1981) using a systems approach. *Journal of Systems Analysis*, 14: 99–109.

Robinson, B. (1994) '... *And treat those two imposters just the same': Analysing systems failure as a social process.* Working paper, Information Technology Institute, University of Salford.

The Royal Academy of Engineering and The British Computer Society (2004) *The Challenges of Complex IT Projects.* www.raeng.org.uk.

Sauer, C. (1993) *Why Information Systems Fail: A Case Study Approach.* Alfred Waller, Henley on Thames.

Turner, B. (1979) *Man-Made Disasters.* Taylor & Francis, London.

White, D. (2003) *A systems view of project management risk.* PhD Thesis, The Open University.

Yap, C.S., Soh, C.P.P. & Raman, K.S. (1992) Information systems success factors in small business. *OMEGA*, 20: 597–609.

INDEX